THE Principal AS Curriculum Leader

2ND EDITION

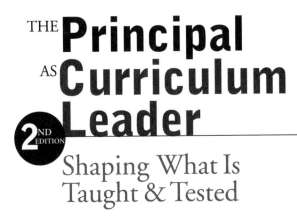

THE **Principal**
AS **Curriculum**
Leader

2ND
EDITION

Shaping What Is
Taught & Tested

Allan A. Glatthorn

CORWIN PRESS, INC.
A Sage Publications Company
Thousand Oaks, California

For information:

CORWIN
PRESS

Corwin Press, Inc.
A Sage Publications Company
2455 Teller Road
Thousand Oaks, California 91320
E-mail: order@corwin.sagepub.com

Sage Publications Ltd.
6 Bonhill Street
London EC2A 4PU
United Kingdom

Sage Publications India Pvt. Ltd.
M-32 Market
Greater Kailash I
New Delhi 110 048 India

Printed in the United States of America

Library of Congress Cataloging-in-Publication Data

Glatthorn, Allan A., 1924-
    The principal as curriculum leader: Shaping what is taught and tested / by Allan A. Glatthorn.— 2nd ed.
        p. cm.
    Includes bibliographical references and index.
    ISBN 0-7619-7556-X (cloth: alk. paper)
    ISBN 0-7619-7557-8 (pbk.: alk. paper)
    1. Curriculum planning—United States. 2. School principals—United States. 3. Educational leadership—United States. 4. School management and organization—United States. I. Title. LB2806.15 .G588 2000
    375'.001—dc21   00-008950

This book is printed on acid-free paper.

01 02 03 10 9 8 7 6 5 4 3 2

Corwin Editorial Assistant: Kylee Liegl
Production Editor: Nevair Kabakian
Editorial Assistant: Cindy J. Bear
Typesetter/Designer: Barbara Burkholder

Contents

Preface

This second edition of the book provides me with an opportunity to update the book to reflect current developments and to strengthen sections that in retrospect needed greater attention. Both opportunities have been seized. To begin with, the book includes recent research related to curriculum and its implementation.

Also, the treatment of several topics has been expanded. This current work gives greater attention to the importance of curriculum (or content) standards, because state standards seem to have become institutionalized in practice. Second, the discussion of how teachers can reduce the gap between the taught curriculum and the learned curriculum has been greatly expanded, because several principals and teachers have requested more specific information about this vital concern. The analysis of the hidden curriculum has been added. Because principals report that they continue to be overwhelmed with noncurricular tasks, a discussion of how to find time for curriculum leadership has been added to the final chapter. Finally, the need for team leadership is so apparent that this topic receives greater attention throughout this work.

Written specifically for school principals, this book is derived from several tested beliefs. The first is that there is no single right way to do curriculum. What is offered here, instead, are some useful guidelines tested in practice, not rigid prescriptions. Principals are strongly encouraged to use the guidelines flexibly. The second is that developing and implementing effective curricula are cooperative ventures in which district leaders, school administrators, and classroom teachers work together toward a common goal. Although this work focuses on the role of the principal, the assumption throughout is that the principal functions as a key player on a cooperative team. The third strong conviction is the need for the principal to play an active leadership role. Unfortunately, that role has been largely ignored in the literature on educational leadership. If students are to succeed through mastery of a quality curriculum, then the principal must play an active role—at all levels, in all stages.

The book reflects these basic beliefs. Part I begins with three chapters that provide a foundation for what is to come by reviewing the knowledge base, examining the four levels of curriculum work, and analyzing the nature and importance of the principal's role.

Part II explains how the principal can influence the state and the district curricula as they are being developed. Part III focuses on the school's curriculum; the argument here is that each school should have its own distinctive curriculum, while still ensuring effective delivery of the district curriculum. Part IV examines the classroom curriculum and explains how the principal can work with teachers in making the classroom curriculum operational and meaningful. In Part V, the book closes with a chapter on practical ways of implementing leadership skills.

The book owes much to several individuals. First, I acknowledge my indebtedness to all the principals with whom I have worked. I feel a special indebtedness to the principals of the Littleton (Colorado) public schools, who generously shared their experiential wisdom. Second, my graduate students at East Carolina University have always taught me a great deal about the realities of schools. The Principal Fellows of 1995-97 were especially helpful in bringing to bear on these issues their considerable experience. Dean Casello, of the Raccoon School in Aliquippa (Pennsylvania), was good enough to read the manuscript and give me constructive feedback. Gracia Alkema, president of Corwin Press, provided very useful guidance at the outset of this project. Finally, I dedicate this book to my family—my children, my wife, and my brothers and sisters; they have always provided the continuing support I need.

Acknowledgments

Corwin Press would like to acknowledge the following reviewers:

Harvey Alvy
Singapore American School
Republic of Singapore

John C. Daresh
University of Texas—El Paso
El Paso, TX

Dennis Dunklee
George Mason University
Fairfax, VA

Roger Kaufman
Florida State University
Tallahassee, FL

Pearl Solomon
St. Thomas Aquinas College
Sparkill, NY

About the Author

Allan A. Glatthorn is Distinguished Research Professor at East Carolina University, Greenville, North Carolina. He formerly was a member of the faculty at the University of Pennsylvania Graduate School of Education. He also served for 26 years as a classroom teacher, district supervisor, and high school principal. He is the author of more than 20 professional books on supervision and curriculum, including *Quality Teaching Through Professional Development,* coauthored with Linda Fox and published by Corwin Press. He has consulted with more than 200 school districts, assisting them in developing and implementing their curricula.

PART

Laying the Foundations

1

What It Means to Be a Curriculum Leader

Principals can best discharge their leadership role if they develop a deep and broad knowledge base with respect to curriculum. This chapter aids in that process by first reviewing current trends in curricula and then summarizing the research on curricular quality.

Current Trends in Curricula

It is sometimes difficult to distinguish significant trends that are likely to be influential for several years from passing fads that will soon disappear. However, a review of the past history of the field and an analysis of the current literature suggest that the following developments are likely to be influential in the first decade of the 21st century.

Increasing Importance of National and State Standards

At the time of this writing, there was still considerable debate about the desirability of standards at the national level. However, the continuing dissatisfaction with the public schools expressed in the national media probably will place pressure on Congress to develop policies that will effect some standardization while still giving primary authority to the states. In a well-balanced analysis, Smith, Fuhrman, and O'Day (1994) summarize the pros and cons of national standards. They cite several advantages claimed by advocates of national standards: Such standards will ensure that all citizens will have the shared knowledge and values needed to make democracy work; they result in greater efficiency because they provide standards for the 50 states; they encourage state and local boards to raise their standards; they will improve the quality of schooling; and they will ensure a large measure of educational equity. It should also be noted here that there is some evidence from international comparisons that teachers in nations with strong central control of the curriculum reported greater consistency about what should be taught and what they did teach, when compared with teachers in nations with greater local control (Cohen & Spillane, 1992). That variation in consistency is probably one of the factors accounting for international differences in achievement.

However, Smith and colleagues (1994) also note several disadvantages emphasized by the critics of the movement toward a national curriculum: Past experience suggests that such attempts will not be effective; standards tend to become minimum standards that lower the entire system; the development at the national level will draw resources from state and local efforts; they can lead to an excessively restrictive national curriculum that will inhibit local creativity; and standards alone will have no effect on student achievement unless significant resources are provided to local school systems (an unlikely development in a time of attempts to downsize the federal government).

Although there is a debate about national standards, there seems to be a growing consensus on the desirability of state standards. A survey by Pechman and Laguarda (1993) indicated that 45 states had developed or were developing curriculum frameworks. And those frameworks seemed to be moving from very general guidelines to more prescriptive mandates and are typically accompanied by state-developed tests. Smith and colleagues (1994) report that preliminary results from California suggest that "ambitious content standards reinforced by assessment and other policies have the potential to improve schooling" (p. 21). The evidence on teacher attitudes is somewhat inconclusive. Two studies suggest that most teachers have negative attitudes about externally imposed curriculum standards (McNeil, 1986; Rosenholtz, 1987). On the other hand, a study of teachers in six states discovered little evidence that teachers were unhappy with state and district standard setting (Porter, Smithson, & Osthoff, 1994). This finding is supported by more recent research indicating that the teacher-authors seemed to accept state standards with a sense of grim resignation (Glatthorn & Fontana, in press).

Several experts have noted problems with state standard setting in curriculum (see especially Fuhrman, 1994). The standards are set by state officials who are far removed from local schools and free of the burden of accountability. Curriculum standards are often not supported with other systemic changes, such as new approaches to teacher education. Thus, state initiatives are typically fragmented and often contradictory. And in a time of limited resources and the accompanying downsizing of state staff, most state departments of education do not have the resources to assist local districts in implementing state standards.

This is an appropriate place to clarify some terms used by most of the states in their publications and in this book.

- *Curriculum standards or content standards.* Statements of what the learner is expected to be able to do, in one subject, grades K-12

  Example (language arts): Uses the reading process to analyze and understand types of literary texts.

- *Benchmarks.* A more specific component of a standard, usually specified for a particular grade or a grade level

  Example (language arts, grades 6-8): Understands the features of myths.

- *Objectives.* A component of a benchmark, usually the focus of a given lesson

  Example (language arts, grade 6): Identifies the features of a mythical hero.

What should the principal do about state standards? The practical response is to help teachers accept them as a part of their professional work, noting both the advantages and disadvantages of externally imposed standards.

Movement Toward School-Based
Curriculum Development

At the same time there is increased interest in national and state standard setting in curriculum, educators have reported growing interest in school-based curriculum development, as one element of the movement toward school-based management. Most schools reporting successful school-based management programs indicated that teachers used their decision-making authority to change the program of studies by adding new courses (U.S. General Accounting Office, 1994). Although one would expect that the concurrent interest in schools of choice would result in greater curricular diversity, one study concluded that there were no major differences between the curriculum found in schools of choice and that found in standard schools (Sosniak & Ethington, 1992). Perhaps more diversity in curriculum will be found in the charter school movement, because charter schools are free of state curriculum control.

Greater Influence of
Professional Organizations

In previous decades, practitioners did not seem to give much attention to the curriculum recommendations of professional groups such as the National Council of Teachers of English. Those recommendations often seemed too radical, insensitive to the realities of classroom life. In the past 10 years, however, the cry for higher standards seems to have given such recommendations greater credence. Almost all the professional associations representing educators in a particular subject field have published their own curriculum standards.

A systematic compilation of those standards by Kendall and Marzano (1997) indicates that those professional standards, viewed collectively, represent an almost impossible task for curriculum leaders. According to their statistics, a student would have to master three "benchmarks" every week to achieve all the standards set by the professional groups. (A *benchmark* is a grade-specific and subject-specific standard.) Principals should become familiar with professional standards but encourage developers to use them selectively. If the school uses subject-centered teams, the principal should also help team leaders stay current about professional standards.

Continuing Interest in
Constructivist Curriculum

Constructivism is a theory of learning based on the principle that learners construct meaning from what they experience; thus, learning is an active, meaning-making process. Though constructivism seems to have made its strongest impact on science and mathematics curricula, leaders in other fields are attempting to embody in curriculum units the following principles.

- The unit should be problem focused, requiring the student to solve open-ended contextualized problems.
- The unit should enable the student to access generative knowledge in solving those problems. Generative knowledge is knowledge that is used in solving problems.

- Learning strategies (such as the use of matrices in organizing information) should be taught in the context of solving problems.
- Throughout the unit, the teacher should provide the necessary scaffolding or structure.
- Much of the learning should occur in cooperative groups, because
  learning is a social process.
- The unit should conclude by requiring the student to demonstrate
  learning in some authentic manner.

Chapter 13 provides a detailed explanation of the processes to be used in
developing a constructivist unit. Two sources are useful if greater depth is
needed: Glatthorn (1994a) and Wiggins and McTighe (1998).

Development of New Approaches
in Vocational Education

In the face of drastic changes in the economy, the workplace, and the
workforce, forward-looking career educators are moving toward new
approaches to curricula. Two developments seem significant.

An Emphasis on Generic Skills

Though almost all career educators see a continuing need to train students in career-specific skills so that they can gain employment after graduation, there is increased interest in so-called generic skills that are not job
specific but instead are general transferable skills that can be used in
almost any career. Perhaps one of the best formulations of these generic
skills is that produced by Stasz, McArthur, Lewis, and Ramsey (1990).
Their formulation is shown in Table 1.1. As can be seen by reviewing this
list (or any other such list), the intent is to equip all students with skills that
will enable them to function in a changing economy and a changing
workplace.

An Emphasis on Integrating Academic
and Career Education

In an attempt to reduce or eliminate the dysfunctional barriers between
academic and career curricula, experts in the field are attempting to bring
about a greater integration of the two. Eight models of integration have
been identified by Grubb, Davis, and Lum (1991); the seven most frequently used models are described briefly in the following.

TABLE 1.1 Generic Skills for a Changing Workplace

Basic skills

  Reading with comprehension and critical judgment

  Writing clearly and effectively

  Mastering mathematical computations

  Performing practical life skills (such as reading a schedule or filling out an application)

  Learning how to learn

Complex reasoning and information-processing skills (presented as a problem-solving process)

  Recognizing a problem

  Analyzing that problem

  Generating solution paths

  Evaluating solution paths and monitoring implementation

  Repairing: using alternative actions

  Reflecting: about the process and the solution

Attitudes and dispositions

  Ability to make decisions

  Willingness to take responsibility for one's decisions

  Willingness to be bold in decision making

  Learning the parameters of the workplace

  Cooperating with others

SOURCE: Adapted and paraphrased from Stasz, McArthur, Lewis, and Ramsey (1990).

1. *Incorporating more academic content in career courses.* Career instructors incorporate into their courses such academic content as reading, writing, science, and mathematics. This has always been done informally by career teachers; there is current interest in developing more systematic models.

2. *Combining career and academic teachers on a teaching team.* In some area career schools, one math teacher and one English teacher will join a team of career teachers, presenting special lessons, working with individual students in a pull-out remedial program, teaching an applied class, and developing materials for the career teachers that reinforce related academic skills.

3. *Making the academic curriculum more career relevant.* Academic teachers incorporate career applications wherever desirable: reading literature about work, using job-related writing exercises, using job-related examples from occupational areas. In some cases this approach is more formalized in the development and implementation of so-called applied academics courses. Three of the most widely used are Principles of Technology (an applied physics course), Applied Mathematics, and Applied Communication. New courses in applied chemistry, applied biology, and materials science and technology are being developed.

4. *Aligning the curricula.* This approach coordinates or aligns closely the content of the career courses and the academic courses; the links between the two fields are strengthened and more clearly delineated. Some use "bridge" assignments that require the student to complete a project that integrates career and academic knowledge.

5. *Using the senior project as a form of integration.* Some schools are using the senior project as a form of integration. In one school, for example, the student's project consists of a written report, a physical representation of some sort (usually completed in the vocational shop), and an oral presentation.

6. *Developing an "academy" model.* Academies usually operate as schools-within-schools. Usually, four teachers collaborate in an academy—one in math, one in English, one in science, and one in the career specialty that is the core of the academy (such as electronics). Other subjects are taken in the regular high school as electives. The teachers work with each other and a single group of students over a multiyear period. The academies establish close ties with local businesses and industries.

7. *Developing occupational high schools and magnet schools.* These magnet schools are similar to the academy, except that they are schoolwide. Examples are Aviation High School in New York and the High School for Health Professions in Houston.

Rather than worrying whether they have the "right" kind of program, principals should evaluate their own programs against the following criteria:

- Does the program of studies open doors for all students, not limit opportunities? In too many cases, obsolete vocational programs did not include the academic subjects required for college admissions.
- Do all students have access to reliable career counseling? In many situations, the counseling is not timely, with students being required to make a program choice in grade 9, when such choices are very unstable.
- Do school administrators and teachers make it clear that there are no second-class programs? They should scrupulously avoid making disparaging comments about vocational education but accord the same respect as they do to academic programs.

Development of Integrated Curricula

Educators seem especially interested in the development and use of curriculum integration as a means of increasing student interest and student knowledge (see Beane, 1995, for a current review). Though the concept of curriculum integration is used to mean a variety of approaches, it is used here to denote the development of curriculum units that combine content from two or more disciplines. Though the research generally supports the use of integrated curricula, some problems are associated with their use (see Chapter 9 for a fuller discussion of the research here). For that reason it is recommended that each school decide to what extent and in what ways it will integrate its curriculum. Chapter 9 suggests a process for making that decision.

Institutionalization of Technology

Some educators continue to question the extensive use of the computer and other technological aids (see, for example, Apple, 1988). However, the use of the computer to manage the curriculum and to facilitate student learning is by this time so widely accepted by schools that the issue is moot. Except for the critics of technology, there is general agreement among educators that the use of sophisticated technology will continue to increase in the schools. (For a recent report, see Baker, 1999.)

The Hallmarks of Curriculum Quality

What constitutes a quality curriculum? In one sense, the question cannot be answered empirically because the question deals so much with values. If principals believe that a narrowly focused curriculum that deals only with the "basics" is most desirable, they will argue for the merits of such a curriculum. On the other hand, if they believe in a comprehensive curriculum that deals broadly with life-related issues, they will advocate that approach. Such a division cannot be reconciled by turning to the research.

If that value issue is put aside, several guidelines for developing a quality curriculum are supported by sound research.

1. *Structure the curriculum so that it results in greater depth and less superficial coverage.* Several studies conclude that focusing in depth on a smaller number of skills and concepts will lead to greater understanding and retention and will also be more supportive of efforts to teach problem solving and critical thinking (e.g., Brophy, 1990; Knapp & Associates, 1991; McDonnell, 1989).

2. *Structure the curriculum so that it focuses on problem solving.* Though the initial interest in critical thinking led many innovators to teach isolated "thinking skills," the research in cognitive psychology indicates clearly that such skills are better learned and retained when they are embedded in problem-solving units that deal with complex meaningful problems, situated in a context. (For more detailed discussion of this issue, see the volume edited by Resnick & Klopfer, 1989.)

3. *Structure and deliver the curriculum so that it facilitates the mastery of essential skills and knowledge of the subjects.* For many years, educators foolishly argued about the primacy of content and process. Recent advances in cognitive psychology indicate clearly that such a dichotomy is dysfunctional. Students can solve complex problems in science, for example, only when they have a deep knowledge base; but that knowledge base must become generative, not inert, when it is actively processed and used in solving meaningful problems (see Minstrell, 1989).

4. *Structure the curriculum so that it is closely coordinated.* Several types of coordination seem important: coordination of content, from grades K-12; coordination of the curriculum for one subject, from September to June; coordination within a unit, so that Lesson 3 builds on Lessons 1 and 2 and leads to Lesson 4; and coordination between two related subjects, such as science and mathematics (Cotton, 1995).

5. *Organize the curriculum so that it provides for multiyear sequential study, not "stand-alone" courses.* Though there may be some value in offering stand-alone courses for enrichment purposes at all levels, McDonnell's (1989) research stresses that multiyear sequential curricula will have greater payoff than single fragmented courses.

6. *Emphasize both the academic and the practical.* Johnson (1989) makes this point about the science curriculum: "Generating concepts in the mind . . . should be related where possible to familiar experiences. Experience is the application of understanding" (p. 9). This linking of the academic and the applied should occur throughout the curriculum, not just in "tech prep" courses.

7. *Develop effective integrated curricula.* As noted above, the extent and nature of such integration should be resolved at the school level.

8. *Focus on the mastery of a limited number of essential curriculum objectives rather than trying to cover too many* (Cotton, 1995). Distinguish between those objectives that require specific grade placement, explicit teaching, and systematic assessment and those that should be nurtured on every suitable occasion (Glatthorn, 1994b) (see Chapter 5 for fuller detail here).

References

Apple, M. W. (1988). Teaching and technology: The hidden effects of computers on teachers and students. In L. E. Beyer & M. W. Apple (Eds.), *The curriculum* (pp. 289-311). Albany: State University of New York Press.

Baker, E. L. (1999). *Technology: Something's coming—something good.* Los Angeles: National Center for Research on Evaluation, Standards, and Student Testing.

Beane, J. A. (1995). *Toward a coherent curriculum.* Alexandria, VA: Association for Supervision and Curriculum Development.

Brophy, J. (1990). Teaching social studies for understanding and higher-order applications. *Elementary School Journal, 90,* 351-417.

Cohen, D. K., & Spillane, J. P. (1992). Policy and practice: The relations between governance and instruction. In G. Grant (Ed.), *Review of research in education.* (Vol. 18, pp. 3-50). Washington, DC: American Educational Research Association.

Cotton, K. (1995). *Effective schooling practice: A research synthesis 1995 update.* Portland, OR: Northwest Regional Educational Laboratory.

Fuhrman, S. H. (1994). Legislatures and education policy. In R. F. Elmore & S. H. Fuhrman (Eds.), *The governance of curriculum* (pp. 30-55). Alexandria, VA: Association for Supervision and Curriculum Development.

Glatthorn, A. A. (1994a). Constructivism: Implications for curriculum. *International Journal of Educational Reform, 3,* 449-455.

Glatthorn, A. A. (1994b). *Developing the quality curriculum.* Alexandria, VA: Association for Supervision and Curriculum Development.

Glatthorn, A. A., & Fontana, J. (in press). *Teachers' views of standards and tests.* Washington, DC: National Education Association.

Grubb, W. N., Davis, G., & Lum, J. (1991). *The cunning hand, the cultured mind: Models for integrating vocational and academic education.* Berkeley, CA: National Center for Research in Vocational Education.

Johnson, J. R. (1989). *Technology.* Washington, DC: American Association for the Advancement of Science.

Kendall, J. S., & Marzano, R. J. (1997). *The systematic identification and articulation of content standards and benchmarks, 1997 update.* Aurora, CO: Mid-continent Regional Educational Laboratory.

Knapp, M. S., & Associates. (1991). *What is taught, and how, to the children of poverty.* Washington, DC: U.S. Department of Education.

McDonnell, L. M. (1989). *Restructuring American schools: The promise and the pitfalls.* New York: Teachers College, Columbia University Institute on Education and the Economy.

McNeil, L. M. (1986). *Contradictions of control.* New York: Routledge & Kegan Paul.

Minstrell, J. A. (1989). Teaching science for understanding. In L. B. Resnick & L. E. Klopfer (Eds.), *Toward the thinking curriculum: Current cognitive research* (pp. 129-149). Alexandria, VA: Association for Supervision and Curriculum Development.

Pechman, E. M., & Laguarda, K. G. (1993). *Status of new state curriculum frameworks, standards, assessments, and monitoring systems.* Washington, DC: Policy Studies Associates.

Porter, A. C., Smithson, J., & Osthoff, E. (1994). Standard setting as a strategy for upgrading high school mathematics and science. In R. F. Elmore & S. H. Fuhrman (Eds.), *The governance of curriculum* (pp. 138-166). Alexandria, VA: Association for Supervision and Curriculum Development.

Resnick, L. B., & Klopfer, L. E. (Eds.). (1989). *Toward the thinking curriculum: Current cognitive research.* Alexandria, VA: Association for Supervision and Curriculum Development.

Rosenholtz, S. J. (1987). Education reform strategies: Will they increase teacher commitment? *American Journal of Education, 95,* 557-559.

Smith, M. S., Fuhrman, S. H., & O'Day, J. (1994). National curriculum standards: Are they desirable and feasible? In R. F. Elmore & S. H. Fuhrman (Eds.), *The governance of curriculum* (pp. 12-29). Alexandria, VA: Association for Supervision and Curriculum Development.

Sosniak, L. A., & Ethington, C. A. (1992). When public school "choice" is not academic: Findings from the National Education Longitudinal Study of 1988. *Educational Evaluation and Policy Analysis, 14,* 35-52.

Stasz, C., McArthur, D., Lewis, M., & Ramsey, K. (1990). *Teaching and learning generic skills for the workplace.* Berkeley, CA: National Center for Research in Vocational Education.

U.S. General Accounting Office. (1994). *Education reform: School-based management results in changes in instruction and budgeting* (No. 15). Washington, DC: Author.

Wiggins, G., & McTighe, J. (1998). *Understanding by design.* Alexandria, VA: Association for Supervision and Curriculum Development.

2

The Four Curriculum Levels: State, District, School, and Classroom

A cold war is being conducted over the control of curriculum. As noted in the previous chapter, state departments of education are becoming much more active in the area of curriculum, developing detailed standards and high-stakes tests based on those standards. At the same time, as indicated in Chapter 1, schools using site-based management are using their authority to develop their own curriculum. Districts continue to assert their authority over the curriculum. And classroom teachers close the door and teach what they wish to teach.

Rather than siding with one of these claimants for control, this book argues for cooperation among the four levels, based on the belief that each has a part to play. As Fuhrman and Elmore (1990) point out, curriculum work is performed most effectively when each of the levels exercises its legitimate role in a collaborative manner. If principals understand the functions at each level, they can provide effective leadership in their schools. There is evidence that principals understand that curriculum making is a multilevel process. A survey of principals conducted by the National Center for Education Statistics (1995) indicated that public school principals felt that four groups had a "great deal" of influence over curriculum: 61% believed that state departments had a great deal of influence; 46%, the school board; 49%, the principal; and 51%, the faculty. Only 7% believed that parents had great influence.

As an overview for what follows in this chapter, Table 2.1 summarizes the functions recommended for each level. Note that Table 2.1 serves also as an organizer for Chapters 6 through 15. Obviously the allocation of these functions should be reviewed closely. Even though the allocations are based on my knowledge of the literature and my experience in consulting with personnel at all four levels, the specific functions undertaken at each level should be determined by state officials, district leaders, principals, and teachers through consultation and dialogue.

State Functions

Four functions should be performed at the state level. The first is the development of *curriculum frameworks.* The term is used here in this sense: a set of statements guiding the development and implementation of curricula and the assessment of student achievement.

Disagreement exists, of course, with respect to the nature and components of state frameworks. Curry and Temple (1992) criticize "traditional" frameworks for the following reasons: They are too traditional in content and perspective; they are too prescriptive; their elements are not related to each other; they do not address systemic reform; they are too linear and lockstep; and they are presented in a "top-down" mode. In the place of such traditional frameworks, they propose "progressive" frameworks that are characterized by the following features: They emphasize a new view of how students learn; they support integration of all components of the curriculum. They argue for comprehensive frameworks that may include all of the following components: philosophy/rationale/goals, learner and school outcomes, content standards, assessment/student performance standards, themes and concepts of the disciplines, professional development/instructional strategies, instructional technology strategies, sample programs/curriculum units, instructional materials criteria, interdisciplinary strategies.

I recommend instead more limited frameworks that include only three elements: (a) the broad educational goals that schools are expected to achieve through all programs in 13 years of schooling, (b) graduation requirements in terms of credits and competencies, and (c) general standards for each required subject. This minimal and general approach is recommended for several reasons. Such an approach gives districts greater autonomy in responding to local needs and strengths, while providing

TABLE 2.1 Summary of Curriculum Functions

State functions

    Develop state frameworks, including broad goals, general standards, and graduation requirements.

    Develop state tests and other performance measures in required academic subjects.

    Provide needed resources to local districts.

    Evaluate state frameworks.

District functions

    Develop and implement curriculum-related policies.

    Develop a vision of a quality curriculum.

    Develop educational goals based on state goals.

    Identify a common program of studies, the curriculum requirements, and subject time allocations, for each level of schooling.

    For each subject, develop the documents for the core or mastery curriculum, including scope and sequence charts and curriculum guides.

    Select instructional materials.

    Develop district curriculum-based tests and other performance measures to supplement state tests.

    Provide fiscal and other resources needed at the school level, including technical assistance.

    Evaluate the curriculum.

School functions

    Develop the school's vision of a quality curriculum, building on the district's vision.

    Supplement the district's educational goals.

    Develop its own program of studies.

    Develop a learning-centered schedule.

    Determine nature and extent of curriculum integration.

    Align the curriculum.

    Monitor and assist in the implementation of the curriculum.

Classroom functions

    Develop yearly planning calendars.

    Develop units of study.

    Enrich the curriculum and remediate learning.

    Evaluate the curriculum.

---

sufficient guidance from the state perspective. It also seems to facilitate district development. My experience in working with numerous districts in several states suggests that very comprehensive state frameworks are often confusing and counterproductive. Finally, the minimal approach is more efficient in relation to the optimal use of state resources at a time of downsizing in public agencies.

The second key function of the state is to develop and implement tests and other performance measures. Again a limited approach is recommended. States should focus their assessment efforts on the following academic subject areas: English language arts, including reading and writing; social studies; science; and mathematics. And assessment should be limited to the three transition points: grades 5, 8, and 12. Such a limited approach would give state officials, district leaders, and the public sufficient information to make major decisions, without devoting too much time and energy on testing. One major study of the impact of statewide minimum competency assessments concluded that such tests reward harmful instructional practices (such as retention and misuse of special education placement) while not encouraging school improvement (Allington & McGill-Franzen, 1992).

In designing and implementing such assessment systems, both state and local leaders should make appropriate use of authentic assessments. At the present time, there is widespread interest in moving from paper-and-pencil objective tests to such alternative measures as demonstrations of learning, projects, open-ended problem solving, and portfolios. In their review of the research on portfolios, Herman and Winters (1994) concluded that assessment portfolios held much promise—if developers achieved high levels of technical quality, if educators ensured that the results were not used to perpetuate inequities, and if the developers and users confronted honestly the demands that authentic assessment placed on evaluators, principals, and teachers. Also, the state should provide school districts with the resources needed to develop and implement quality curricula. Adequate fiscal resources and effective technical assistance seem to be the most important.

Finally, state frameworks should be carefully evaluated while they are being produced and after they have been disseminated. Reviewers should consider both professional soundness and feasibility.

District Functions

Each district needs a consistent program of studies for each level of schooling and a uniform curriculum for each subject. Such consistency and standardization has several advantages. First, it ensures equity across the district. All students receive a quality curriculum, regardless of the school they attend. Second, it facilitates student mobility; students can transfer within the district, confident that they will not be penalized because they have missed important content. Third, the district curriculum is more likely to ensure coordination from level to level. If each school is left to its own devices, breaks in continuity can be expected. And as Cotton (1995) notes, such coordination contributes significantly to student achievement.

District development of the K through 12 curriculum does not preclude school-based curriculum development. In the model advocated here, the district should develop a *mastery core* curriculum. The mastery core first specifies the subjects that all schools will offer at each grade. Second, for each of those subjects, the mastery core defines the essential skills and knowledge that require explicit teaching and careful structuring. Then, to enable each school to develop its own curriculum, the district should make supplementary funds available so that every school can add courses that will enable it to respond to the unique needs of its students.

In identifying the mastery core for each subject, subject matter task forces should develop a sharply focused curriculum that does not require more than 80% of available time for all students to master. The remaining time is then available for teachers to add their own enrichment.

In achieving this goal of a quality curriculum for all students, district leaders should accomplish the tasks identified in Table 2.1 and explained in Chapter 5.

School Functions

Now the school takes over. Under the leadership of the principal and teacher leaders and with appropriate input from parents, the school develops its own curriculum that will build on the district mastery core. The faculty develop their own vision, identify their own goals, and supplement the district-mandated program by adding courses that respond to the special needs of their students. The principal gets input from the teachers in developing a school schedule that will maximize learning opportunities. The faculty determine the extent and nature of curriculum integration. They collaborate in aligning the curriculum and monitoring the implementation of the curriculum.

Thus, there is much important work for the school to do, under the leadership of an informed and active principal.

Classroom Functions

Finally, the classroom teachers operationalize the curriculum in several critical ways. Obviously, they can do this either as individuals or as mem-

TABLE 2.2 Allocation of Functions

REVISED FUNCTIONS	STATE	DISTRICT	SCHOOL	CLASSROOM
Develop state frameworks	X			
Develop state tests	X			
Develop educational goals	X	X	X	
Identify common program of studies		X		
Develop mastery core curriculum		X		

bers of a team or department. They work together in teams to build yearly planning calendars and then develop units of study based on that calendar. They enrich the curriculum, adding to the district curriculum special content that responds to their students' needs and enables them to use their own special knowledge. They remediate learning as the need arises. And then they implement that enriched curriculum. They also evaluate the curriculum, bringing to bear their own special perspectives.

Flexible Allocations

Although the suggested allocations shown in Table 2.1 should work for most school systems, they would certainly not apply to all. It therefore makes sense for principals to cooperate with district leaders in the allocation of functions that will better reflect the resources available.

With input from teachers, district and school leaders can use this process:

1. Strike out any function that does not seem important for that district.
2. Add any functions that have not been listed.
3. Indicate on a form similar to the one shown in Table 2.2 those functions that the state actually performs. (Table 2.2 shows only a portion of the functions that would be listed.)
4. Allocate the remaining to the other three levels in a manner responsive to resources and needs. This allocation should result from extensive dialog and analysis that include district staff, school administrators, and teachers.

A Concluding Note

The cold war over the control of the curriculum can be ended by respect for the authority of each level, cooperation across the levels, and systematic planning.

References

Allington, R. L., & McGill-Franzen, A. (1992). Does high-stakes testing improve school effectiveness? *ERS Spectrum, 10*(2), 3-12.
Cotton, K. (1995). *Effective schooling practices: A research synthesis, 1995 update.* Portland, OR: Northwest Regional Educational Laboratory.

Curry, B., & Temple, T. (1992). *Using curriculum frameworks for systemic reform.* Alexandria, VA: Association for Supervision and Curriculum Development.

Fuhrman, S. H., & Elmore, R. F. (1990). Understanding local control in the wake of state education reform. *Educational Evaluation and Policy Analysis, 12,* 82-96.

Herman, J. L., & Winters, L. (1994). Portfolio research: A slim collection. *Educational Leadership, 52*(2), 48-55.

National Center for Education Statistics. (1995). *Who influences decisionmaking about curriculum: What do principals say?* Washington, DC: Author.

3

Importance of the Principal

I f school administrators are to serve as effective leaders of curriculum, they need to understand the importance of this role of the principal. This chapter begins by defining briefly the concept of *curriculum leadership* and notes the problems that face principals in executing this role. The chapter continues by presenting a rationale for its importance and indicating how principal leadership can be joined with teacher leadership for effective collaboration. The chapter concludes by suggesting some specific ways by which the principal can discharge the leadership function.

Defining Curriculum Leadership

The concept of curriculum leadership is used in this book in the following sense:

> The exercise of those functions that enable school systems and their schools to achieve their goal of ensuring quality in what students learn. Several aspects of this definition require attention.

First, the definition emphasizes functions, not roles. Whereas the emphasis of this work is on the role of the principal, several other role incumbents can work together in discharging these responsibilities. Superintendents, assistant superintendents, central office supervisors, principals, assistant principals, department chairs, team leaders, and classroom teachers—all have a part to play.

Second, it emphasizes leadership as those processes that enable systems and individuals to achieve their goals. The functions are goal oriented instead of being a set of steps that are taken mindlessly as routine actions. And the ultimate goal is maximizing student learning by providing quality in the content of learning. Thus, the work makes a simple distinction between curriculum (what is learned) and instruction (how the content is taught).

Understanding the Problems

Several problems confront school administrators interested in discharging this role. The first is lack of clarity about its nature. Principals seem to encounter problems in understanding clearly what it means to be a curriculum leader. In workshops I've conducted, principals have expressed uncertainty about the specific nature of curriculum leadership, often suggesting that curriculum is a district concern, not a school issue.

This attitude of "curriculum is not my job" has perhaps been intensified by the promulgation of state standards. Although state standards and state tests limit the authority of both the district and the school, the argument of this work is that many key functions need to be discharged by the principal and the teachers.

The second difficulty is lack of time. Even when principals are generally aware of their curriculum responsibilities, they have difficulty finding the time to execute the role. One study indicated that high school principals reported that "program development" was first on their list of what they should spend time on—but fourth in terms of time actually spent (Pellicer, Anderson, Keefe, Kelley, & McCleary, 1988).

Finally, principals do not seem to be receiving much help from the experts in understanding curriculum leadership. The literature on the role of the principal as a curriculum leader is surprisingly limited. Though there seem to be hundreds of articles and books dealing with instructional leadership, a recent search of the ERIC database on the leadership role of the principal in curriculum revealed only a small number of sources. It would seem that most experts who have examined school leadership have focused unduly on the principal as a leader of instruction, ignoring the role of curriculum leader. A notable exception here is English's (1992) book.

This book attempts to deal with all these problems. It analyzes systematically the nature of that role, indicates clearly what steps need to be taken in discharging it, and suggests how principals can find time for serving as curriculum leaders.

Understanding the Rationale
for Principal Leadership

Why should the principal serve as a curriculum leader? The answer is based on several tested assumptions. First, a quality curriculum is essential in achieving educational excellence. Though this assumption has the appeal of common sense, it is also supported by sound research. By reviewing more than 3,000 studies of student achievement, Fraser, Walberg, Welch, and Hattie (1987) identified the quality of the curriculum as one of ten factors influencing student achievement (see also Cotton, 1995, for a summary of the research here). The best teaching methods used in delivering poor content result only in a great deal of mislearning.

Second, though both the state and the district have key roles to play in the development and implementation of curricula, there is widespread agreement among the experts that meaningful change takes place primarily at the school level (see, for example, Glickman, 1993; Murphy, 1991; Newmann & Wehlage, 1995). As explained in the previous chapter, the best curriculum work integrates curriculum functions at several levels—state, district, school, and classroom.

Also, there is abundant evidence that the principal plays a key role in determining the overall effectiveness of the school. As will be noted later, teachers can work with the principal collaboratively in discharging these vital leadership functions. However, even in the best teacher leadership models, there is a strong need for the principal to provide ongoing leadership, as noted by Lee, Bryk, and Smith in their 1993 review.

Also Hord and Hall (1983) concluded that strong leadership on the part of the principal played a key role in determining the extent of curriculum leadership. They also discovered that principals who used an active *initiating* style were most effective in ensuring effective implementation. The following attitudes and behaviors characterize this style: (a) have clear long-range policies and goals, (b) have strong expectations for students as well as convey and monitor those expectations, (c) seek changes in district programs and policies, and (d) solicit input from staff but act decisively.

Uniting Principal and Teacher Leadership

There is currently a great deal of interest in implementing models of teacher leadership (see, for example, Bolman & Deal, 1994; Walling,

TABLE 3.1 Analyzing Curriculum Leadership Roles

Directions: **Listed below are the essential functions of curriculum leadership as they should be carried out at the school and classroom levels. For each function, determine what role each of the individuals or groups**[a] **noted on the chart should play. Use this code in responding:**

      L: This individual or group should *lead* in discharging this function.
      C: This individual or group should *contribute* to this function.

Leave the space blank if you believe that this individual or group should play no role at all.

Function	*DS*	*P*	*AP*	*TL*	*T*
School Functions					
1. Develop the school's vision of a quality curriculum, building on the district's vision.					
2. Supplement the district's educational goals.					
3. Develop its own program of studies.					
4. Develop a learning-centered schedule.					
5. Determine nature and extent of curriculum integration.					
6. Align the curriculum.					
7. Monitor and assist in the implementation of the curriculum.					
Classroom Functions					
1. Develop yearly planning calendars for operationalizing the curriculum.					
2. Develop units of study.					
3. Enrich the curriculum and remediate learning.					
4. Evaluate the curriculum.					

a. Code: DS = district supervisor; P = principal; AP = assistant princial; TL = team leaders and department chairs; T = classroom teachers

1994). Unfortunately, most of the models of teacher leadership seem to suggest that it occurs in a vacuum, totally removed from the world of the principal. Wasley's (1991) work is an exception: Her case studies of teacher leaders concluded that administrative support and collaboration are essential if such programs are to be effective.

In support of Wasley's findings, my experience in working with school districts in improving curriculum indicates clearly that leadership in the area of curriculum should be exercised collaboratively and flexibly. The collaboration is essential, because the tasks are manifold and multiple perspectives are vital. Flexibility is crucial, because contextual elements vary so much. To ensure both collaboration and flexibility, the principal and the teachers together should analyze the following factors in determining the balance between principal and teacher leadership:

- The personnel resources available from the central office
- The extent of curriculum work at the district level
- The total responsibilities of the principal
- The other administrative help available to the principal
- The curriculum priorities at the school level
- The extent to which teachers are interested in curriculum leadership
- The time and other resources available to teachers

One way of operationalizing this analysis is to use the form shown in Table 3.1. Observe that the form lists all the functions specified for both the school and the classroom curriculum. (The list presented here should be checked against the master list shown in Table 2.2, to be sure that they are congruent.) The principal should initiate the process by discussing the issues and the process in a general faculty meeting. At that time, the principal can emphasize the importance of collaboration, explain the nature of each function, and clarify how teachers can provide input. (Chapters 6 through 15 provide detailed information with respect to each of these functions.) After this orientation session, the principal should complete the form as indicated and then distribute it to the faculty for them to respond. When all responses have been tallied and summarized, the principal should confer with team leaders (a generic term that includes department chairs) to analyze the results and build the local school model of curricular leadership.

Discharging the Leadership Functions

Once the leadership functions have been delineated, the principal can best discharge those functions by keeping in mind two general recommendations. The first is to use the routine acts that consume the typical day as occasions for curriculum emphasis. Scott, Ahadi, and Krug (1990) determined that principals who were most effective in discharging instructional leadership (which they defined as including curriculum leadership) did not use different behaviors from less effective principals; instead, they used routine behaviors as opportunities for curriculum emphasis and gave their routine actions a curricular interpretation. For example, in monitoring the student cafeteria, they would stop and talk with students about what they were learning and how they felt about their subjects.

The second recommendation is that the principal understand that curriculum leadership does not exist in a vacuum but is simply one component of effective organizational behavior. In their study of effective curriculum leaders, Aronstein and DeBenedictis (1988) determined that such principals used behaviors that had a schoolwide impact rather than a narrowly focused curriculum emphasis. They identified five "enabling behaviors" that made a schoolwide difference: (a) facilitating communication, (b) creating a positive open climate, (c) building a vision with the staff, (d) developing staff through involvement, and (e) being an effective and positive role model. Additional suggestions for operationalizing the principal's role can be found in Chapter 16.

References

Aronstein, L. W., & DeBenedictis, K. L. (1988). *The principal as a leader of curriculum change: A study of exemplary school administrators.* Quincy: Massachusetts State Department of Education.

Bolman, L. G., & Deal, T. E. (1994). *Becoming a teacher leader.* Thousand Oaks, CA: Corwin.

Cotton, K. (1995). *Effective schooling practices: A research synthesis 1995 update.* Portland, OR: Northwest Regional Educational Laboratory.

English, F. W. (1992). *Deciding what to teach and test: Developing, aligning, and auditing the curriculum.* Thousand Oaks, CA: Corwin.

Fraser, B. J., Walberg, H. J., Welch, W. W., & Hattie, J. A. (1987). Syntheses of educational productivity research. *International Journal of Education, 11,* 145-152.

Glickman, C. D. (1993). *Renewing America's schools.* San Francisco: Jossey-Bass.

Hord, S. M., & Hall, G. E. (1983). *Three images: What principals do in curriculum implementation.* Austin: University of Texas, Research and Development Center for Teacher Education.

Lee, V. E., Bryk, A. S., & Smith, J. B. (1993). The organization of effective secondary schools. In L. Darling-Hammond (Ed.), *Review of research in education* (Vol. 19). Washington, DC: American Educational Research Association.

Murphy, J. (1991). *Restructuring schools.* New York: Teachers College Press.

Newmann, F. M., & Wehlage, G. G. (1995). *Successful school restructuring.* Madison: University of Wisconsin, Center on Organization and Restructuring of Schools.

Pellicer, L. O., Anderson, L. W., Keefe, J. W., Kelley, E. A., & McCleary, L. E. (1988). *High school leaders and their schools: Vol. 1. A national profile.* Reston, VA: National Association of Secondary School Principals.

Scott, C., Ahadi, S., & Krug, S. E. (1990). *The experience sampling approach to the study of principal instructional behavior* (Vol. 2). Urbana, IL: National Center for School Leadership.

Walling, D. R. (Ed.). (1994). *Teachers as leaders.* Bloomington, IN: Phi Delta Kappan.

Wasley, P. A. (1991). *Teachers who lead.* New York: Teachers College Press.

PART

*Shaping State and
District Curricula*

4

State Policies
and Frameworks

As explained in Chapter 2, the state has a legitimate role to play in the development of curriculum policies and frameworks. It is here that principals need to be proactive, influencing those foundation documents as they are being developed rather than only responding reactively after they have been finalized. Principals also have a role in evaluating state documents once they have been published. The point of view advanced here is that principals have a professional responsibility to exercise their influence at the state level.

Becoming Informed

The first step is to become informed about state initiatives as they are being developed. Three kinds of information are crucial. First, principals need to keep informed in advance about what new initiatives are developing. Here the state professional association is the best source. Second, they need to understand the political and legislative processes as they operate in their states. That knowledge embraces both the formal processes that are explicated in the law but, even more important, includes the informal processes that really get things done. State policy making operates through informal contacts, through discussions with lobbyists and pressure groups, and through behind-the-scenes negotiating and bargaining.

Finally, they need to be kept informed about the best research on current educational reforms. Principals can speak and write more persuasively if they speak from an informed perspective. The best sources here are the professional journals.

Getting the Message Across

With that knowledge, principals can then work at communicating their views to state legislators and other policymakers. They can do this both as members of professional associations, most of which have their own lobbyists, and as individuals.

In working with professional groups, principals should encourage them to develop and disseminate policy briefings. These are documents written for state and local policymakers on the vital educational issues being examined for possible action (see Glatthorn, 1996, as an example of this type of document, written for North Carolina policymakers on the issue of charter schools). The policy briefings will be most effective if they are objective and unbiased, if they cite the evidence, if they are brief and to the point, and if they are in the hands of legislators immediately prior to their consideration of proposed legislation.

In speaking and writing individually to policymakers, principals should keep in mind certain commonsense guidelines about such communication:

- Say it in your own words. Legislators quickly recognize canned messages.
- Keep the message brief and to the point. Policymakers are busy people; they usually will not read lengthy documents.
- Use a professional tone. Use language that is courteous, respectful, and objective.
- Communicate persuasively. Analyze the values. Examine the issues. Provide the evidence.
- Be sure the form is perfect. Have someone check the letter for spelling, punctuation, and sentence structure.

A letter that exemplifies these qualities is shown in Figure 4.1.

Evaluating State Frameworks

In addition to influencing state policy making in a proactive fashion, principals should also participate in the evaluation of state materials once they

Figure 4.1 Letter to Legislator

Dear Senator Bridges:

I write to you as a constituent and as a concerned educator about Senate Bill 1045, "Authorization of Charter Schools," to be proposed for action during the May special session.

Although the concept of charter schools is potentially an attractive one, I believe that additional study is needed before the state authorizes their establishment. My review of the research raises these concerns.

Will charter schools draw funds from public schools?
Will charter schools be selective and exclusionary?
Will charter schools divert attention from the need to reform public education?
Will charter schools achieve their own objectives of raising student achievement?

I would be happy to provide you with additional information about these issues if you and your colleagues desire it.

I would much appreciate it if you would see fit to vote NO on charter schools.

---

have been developed by state department of education staffs. In assessing state frameworks, the following criteria can be used:

- Do the frameworks represent the best current professional thinking and reflect sound empirical research? (Too many frameworks seem to be excessively responsive to passing fads, such as curriculum integration.)
- Do the frameworks provide a reasonable measure of state direction while still giving local districts sufficient autonomy? (Several state frameworks seem highly controlling and overly specific.)
- Are the state frameworks easy to use at the local level? (Several state frameworks seem excessively complicated, so that they make the work of the local district exceedingly difficult.)

- Are the elements of the state frameworks compatible and coherent? (One state curriculum guide in reading emphasized that each reader brought to bear his or her unique experience in interpreting a literary passage; the state test asked students to choose the "correct" interpretation of a passage from among four alternatives.)
- What is the evidence that the state frameworks will have a significant impact on student learning? (Some state frameworks deal with peripheral elements that will probably not have an impact on student learning.)

Reference

Glatthorn, A. A. (1996). *Policy brief: Charter schools.* Greenville, NC: East Carolina University.

5

District Curricula

Too many principals take a passive, hands-off stance with respect to the district curricula, falsely assuming that the district guides are of little consequence to them. The truth of the matter is that district curricula, if effectively implemented, significantly affect the daily acts of teaching and learning. District curricula, therefore, must become the business of school principals. To increase principal influence on district curricula, this chapter describes briefly each of the district's tasks and then explains how principals can exercise their influence.

District Functions

The nine functions identified in Chapter 2 are explained here. Keep in mind that the balance between district and school functions should be determined locally.

Develop and Implement
Curriculum-Related Policies

Policy making, of course, is the prerogative of the school board. However, in most districts, the board relies on the superintendent to suggest where policies are needed and to frame draft policies that reflect board views. Because policies are critical in providing general directions for the administration of the schools, principals should work through the superintendent to ensure that board policies set a forward-looking direction for the schools.

In his design of a curriculum audit, English (1988) recommends that the board develop policies in the following areas: a planned relationship between the written, the taught, and the tested curricula; test and textbook adoption; and curriculum-related budgeting. In conducting curriculum audits, English now seems to use 22 "characteristics" in determining if policies are adequate (see, for example, Vertiz, 1994). The expanded list includes elements such as curriculum monitoring, staff development, and equal access.

Here is an example of the policy recommended by English and his colleagues in the area of the tested curriculum.

> The district will establish models for determining the effectiveness of instructional programming at district, school, and classroom levels. Evaluations will focus on determining the extent to which students are achieving and maintaining their mastery of appropriate specific learning opportunities and the extent to which instructors are displaying effective conveyance of curriculum in the classrooms. (Vertiz, 1994, p. 286)

Develop a Vision of a Quality Curriculum

I have found it helpful in working with several school districts to assist them in developing their vision of a quality curriculum. The vision becomes a set of guidelines for evaluating all curriculum products. For example, if the vision statement speaks of a curriculum that values diversity, one would expect to see a U.S. history curriculum guide that gives significant attention to the struggle for equity by African Americans. The process of developing a vision is explained briefly here and then discussed more fully in Chapter 6. A group process is recommended, with individuals first working on their own and then sharing the results with the rest of the group. Each person lists 10 adjectives that characterize the vision of curriculum quality and then expands on that adjective with a sentence or two. Here is an example:

Global: The curriculum helps students understand that all nations are interconnected.

Develop the District's Educational Goals

An educational goal is a broad statement of the outcomes the district wants to achieve for all students through the entire educational program, from kindergarten to grade 12. Here is an example of an educational goal:

- Understand mathematical concepts and apply mathematical skills and knowledge in solving problems.

Although Spady and Marshall (1991) recommended "transformational" outcomes that transcended the traditional subjects, several conservative citizen groups complained that outcomes such as "quality producers" were too value-laden and intruded into family responsibilities. As a consequence, most districts that enthusiastically adopted transformational outcomes seem to have backed off, substituting more traditional ones.

Most state frameworks will include goal statements. If the district decides to develop its own, then principals should have significant input into the process. The process of developing goals is more fully explained in Chapter 6.

Develop a Common Program
of Studies for All Students

The program of studies is the collective set of educational experiences offered at a given level of schooling. Thus, typically a school district would have three programs of study—one for elementary, one for middle, and one for high schools. The position here is that the district should define a common mastery core curriculum for all students and then enable individual schools to go beyond the core curriculum by adding special electives. The specification of the program of studies usually includes the following elements:

- Subjects required at each grade level
- Electives offered at each level of schooling
- Recommended time allocations for each subject at each level
- Credits for each subject
- Promotion and graduation requirements

Obviously, the program of studies will reflect state and school board requirements with respect to graduation requirements.

The decision about the scope and nature of the program of studies is crucial, because it affects student learning, budget, facilities, schedules, and staffing. Principals should therefore use every opportunity to influence the district's decisions with respect to the level of schooling for which principals are responsible. Additional information about developing the school's program of studies is provided in Chapter 7.

Develop Documents for the Specific Subject

All the previous documents have applied to the entire program of studies—all the subjects at all levels. District leaders also need to develop plans and processes for developing scope and sequence charts and curriculum guides for the individual subjects. A detailed explanation of the process can be found in my 1994 work (Glatthorn, 1994). Although districts will vary in the processes used, leaders should keep in mind the following guidelines, which have been derived from my experience in working with numerous school districts:

1. Review state frameworks to ensure that district products are compatible.
2. Review the curriculum standards recommended by professional groups.
3. Provide in-depth staff development to inform teachers of standards and trends.
4. Involve informed teachers in recommending benchmarks for their grade level. As explained previously, a *benchmark* is a more specific component of a standard, usually assigned to a grade or a grade level. Here are examples from Kendall and Marzano (1997, paraphrased).

   U.S. history standard: Understands family life now and in the past.

   Benchmark, grades 9-12. Understands how interpretations of Columbus's voyages and his interactions with indigenous peoples have changed.

5. Focus on mastery objectives—those that require explicit teaching, careful structuring, and systematic assessment.
6. Keep the scope of the mastery curriculum limited, so that classroom teachers can enrich the district mastery curriculum.
7. Develop curriculum guides based on the scope and sequence chart.
8. Ensure that all materials are teacher-friendly: focused on mastery and easy to use.

Select Instructional Materials

Only after the mastery curriculum has been developed should the district evaluate and select the instructional materials—the texts, the software, and other media. Even though some districts reverse the process (purchasing basic texts and then developing curriculum from them), the text should serve the curriculum and not drive it. Textbooks in general are not reliable foundations for the curriculum. Principals should exercise their influence to ensure that the district's selection process is systematic and objective. As suggested earlier, the primary criterion is that the text corresponds closely with the district curriculum guide. One simple way of doing this is to note for each objective the specific page numbers in the text that relate to that objective. If there is a close fit, then the selection committee can consider other criteria such as readability, cost, durability, and freedom from bias. A more complex process, termed *curriculum alignment*, can also be used; this process is explained in Chapter 10.

Develop District Curriculum-Based Assessments

Once the curriculum guide has been developed and materials have been selected, the district testing office should proceed to develop the district testing program. This should obviously supplement, not duplicate, the state testing program.

Principals should exercise leadership in ensuring that the district testing program meets the following standards:

- Does not demand excessive amounts of time for administrators, teachers, and students
- Does not require excessive funds in development, administration, and scoring of tests
- Gives educators and parents important information about student achievement
- Provides results in a form that teachers can use and understand
- Uses authentic measures wherever feasible, without relying excessively on paper-and-pencil measures

Several leaders in the field of assessment have expressed caution about the excessive and inappropriate use of tests. Darling-Hammond (1990) raises these concerns about standardized achievement tests: (a) They overemphasize lower-order skills; (b) they exert subtle pressure on teachers to focus on fragmented skills, minimizing teacher creativity; (c) the tasks of preparing for, administering, and recording the results of such tests take away time for "real teaching"; and (d) the results are misused by

TABLE 5.1 Criteria for Evaluating Curriculum Guides

Format and style

The guide is formatted and organized so that it is easy to use and to update: the guide is flexible and "teacher-friendly."

The writing and the appearance of the guide convey an image of high professional quality.

Relationship with other sources

The content of the guide reflects the best current thinking about that subject, as exhibited in both sound research and in the standards developed by professional organizations.

The content of the guide reflects state curriculum standards and state tests.

Focus

The guide focuses on a limited number of key objectives, resulting in greater depth and providing opportunities for teacher enrichment.

Sequence and placement

The grade placement of objectives is developmentally appropriate.

The grade placement of objectives reflects systematic development and coordination from grade to grade, without excessive repetition.

The grade placement of objectives in this subject is articulated with the placement of objectives in related subjects (e.g., the mathematics guide emphasizes the math needed for successful performance in science at a given grade level).

Content

The guide reflects an appropriate recognition of the diversity of this society.

The guide facilitates but does not mandate the integration of content from other subjects.

---

administrators. Principals should keep these concerns in mind as they evaluate and attempt to influence the district testing program.

**Provide Resources
Needed by the Schools**

The district should implement processes that will ensure that each school has the resources it needs to implement curricula effectively. Those resources include funds, personnel, training, and technical assistance. It is especially important that the district budgeting process results in equity among schools, so that all schools have sufficient funds.

Evaluate the Curriculum

The district should have in place a sound plan for evaluating the curriculum.

Documents such as the vision statement and the list of educational goals should be reviewed by the school board, central office staff, school administrators, and school faculties before they are finalized.

Three other evaluations are critical. First, each curriculum guide should be evaluated once it has been completed. Table 5.1 lists criteria that can be used in evaluating the guide. Second, the district should use a pilot test to evaluate how the new guide actually works in practice. Some districts use the first year of implementation as a pilot test. Other districts identify a representative sample of classrooms to test the new curriculum before it is widely disseminated. Regardless of the method used, teachers should have an opportunity to try out the new curriculum and give developers feedback about its effectiveness in the classroom.

Finally, the new curriculum should be evaluated during the first year of full implementation. Teachers should be surveyed about their perceptions of the new curriculum in use. In addition, student achievement should be monitored closely during that first crucial year.

Exercising Principal Influence

Principals can exercise their influence in several ways. First, it is recommended that principals be represented on the district Curriculum Planning Council. This is a district group that develops and monitors a comprehensive plan for developing curriculum guides for all subjects. Second, principals should also be included on every subject matter task force. The task force is the group that develops the curriculum guide for a given subject. Finally, principals should use their informal contacts with district administrators, supervisors, and classroom teachers to influence the direction of curriculum development in their districts.

District staff and teachers will pay greater attention to the principal's curriculum views if the principal is seen as knowledgeable and informed. One useful source here is the work I edited, which includes a chapter on the content of each of the subjects in the curriculum (Glatthorn, 1995).

References

Darling-Hammond, L. (1990). Achieving our goals: Superficial or structural reforms?*Phi Delta Kappan, 72*, 286-295.

English, F. W. (1988). *Curriculum auditing.* Lancaster, PA: Technomic.

Glatthorn, A. A. (1994). *Developing the quality curriculum.* Alexandria, VA: Association for Supervision and Curriculum Development.

Glatthorn, A. A. (1995). *The content of the curriculum* (2nd ed.). Alexandria, VA: Association for Supervision and Curriculum Development.

Kendall, J. S., & Marzano, R. J. (1997). *The systematic identification and articulation of content standards and benchmarks, 1997 update.* Aurora, CO: Mid-continent Regional Educational Laboratory.

Spady, W. G., & Marshall, K. J. (1991). Beyond traditional outcome-based education.- *Edcational Leadership, 48*(2), 67-72.

Vertiz, V. C. (1994). *A curriculum management audit.* Arlington, VA: American Association of School Administrators, National Curriculum Audit Center.

PART

Providing Leadership

6

Developing Vision and Goals

The focus now changes in this and the next five chapters from the district's curriculum to the school's curriculum. This chapter suggests processes by which the school can develop its own curriculum vision and goals. These foundation documents can be very useful at the school level. They provide a unifying focus for the faculty. They give a clear sense of direction for curriculum work. They provide a basis for evaluating curricula. And they provide the occasion for professional dialogue.

Developing the School's Vision of a Quality Curriculum

If the district has developed its own vision of a quality curriculum, the school faculty, under the direction of the principal, can simply supplement the district vision. The easiest way to accomplish this task is for the faculty to meet in small groups to answer this question: What features should make the curriculum of our school unique? Each group should attempt to identify three adjectives that capture the specialness of the school's curriculum. The principal can then synthesize the results from each group, identifying six factors most frequently mentioned by the small groups. Each group should then discuss the six factors. Following that discussion, each individual should identify no more than three of those six factors that he or she considers essential for the school's vision. The principal meets with a committee of teachers, using the results to draft a tentative version of the school's vision. The draft is then reviewed by the faculty.

Here is an example that a middle school with a technology emphasis developed:

> We endorse the district's vision of a quality curriculum. In addition, we note these features that we especially hope to embody in our curriculum:

> *Developmentally appropriate.* Because the middle school years are especially important in the cognitive development of young adolescents, we envision a curriculum that gives special attention to the developmental nature of learning.

> *Technologically sophisticated.* As a magnet school emphasizing the educational uses of technology, we envision a curriculum that enables all students to master the technology and to develop a critical perspective about its use.

If the district has not developed its own vision, then the school can use the following more complex process. (This same process can be used by district leaders who wish to develop the vision.)

1. Assemble participants and organize them into groups of six. The participants can include parents, students, and educators.
2. Explain the importance of the vision-making process, stressing its future use in shaping and evaluating curriculum products.
3. Develop the knowledge base for the group by reviewing elements such as the changing society, the characteristics of the community, the nature of the student body, and research on curriculum, teaching, and learning.
4. Explain to the participants that they individually should complete this statement: "I have a dream of a curriculum that is . . ." Without any group discussion, each person should complete the statement by writing 10 adjectives that capture the essence of his or her vision. Here are some examples: *integrated, meaningful, global, technological, goal oriented.*
5. Each person then jots down a sentence or two expanding on the adjective, as in this example:

> *Meaningful:* The curriculum should enable the student to find meaning and purpose in what is being studied; the curriculum should connect with the lives of the learners.

6. The members of each group then share their adjectives and sentences with each other, in round-robin fashion, with the group leader listing the adjectives only on the board.

7. Group members can then ask questions of clarification. Members clarify the meaning of the adjectives by reading their expanding sentences again and explaining any ideas that are unclear.

8. Each person then has three minutes to advocate for one of the adjectives. After the advocacy, each member allocates 15 votes to any of the adjectives listed on the board that he or she believes are important.

9. The group discusses further the entire list to be sure that the adjectives with the largest number of votes are those they support most of all.

10. Each group presents its results to the larger group, and the facilitator of the session helps to identify commonalities and find a consensus.

An example of a curriculum vision is shown in Table 6.1.

The process explained here is my version of the *nominal group process,* which attempts to capture the advantages of both individual and group thinking. Further information about the nominal group process can be found in Moore (1987).

This version of the vision should be seen as an initial tentative framing of desirable characteristics, to be reviewed by all constituencies, including the school board. Once the vision has been developed, the principal should ask the faculty to review it from time to time to ensure that it still represents their ideals. As Fullan (1991) notes, vision building is an interactive, ongoing process, not a one-time event.

Some cautions about vision building should be noted. First, the visioning process need not come first in school improvement.

Some research suggests that in schools that have been improving, the principal and faculty focus on solving problems. After solving several problems, they become aware of an evolving vision. In this sense, the vision emerges from practice. Second, the vision-building process should not become a meaningless exercise. The principal needs to stress the importance of the process. Finally, the vision should be used to guide all the key aspects of the curriculum-making process.

Developing the School's Curriculum Goals

Two goal-related tasks are important in developing the school's curriculum: (a) identifying the educational goals and (b) aligning goals with programs and subjects.

Identifying the Educational Goals

If the district has developed its own goal statement, the school can simply add any goals it considers essential for its program. If goals do not

TABLE 6.1 Washington City Schools' Vision of Curriculum

We, the educators of the Washington City School System, hold forth this vision of the curriculum of excellence we desire for all our students. We have a dream of a curriculum that is . . .

1. Meaningful: The curriculum emphasizes the active construction of meaning so that all students find purpose in their studies.

2. Technological: The curriculum uses technology as one delivery system, examines the influence of technology on students' lives, and gives students the skills they need to use the technology to accomplish their own purposes.

3. Socially responsible: The curriculum develops in students a sense of social responsibility so that they become aware of their obligations and duties as citizens in a democracy and are especially sensitive to the needs of the poor and the aged.

4. Multicultural: The curriculum reflects and is responsive to the cultural diversity of this nation and our community so that students develop a sense of pride in their own heritage and a respect for that of others.

5. Reflective: The curriculum fosters in students the skills and attitudes of reflection so that they are able to think critically, creatively, and affirmatively.

6. Holistic: The curriculum gives appropriate emphasis to all the significant aspects of growth and all the types of human intelligence.

7. Global: The curriculum develops in students an awareness of global interdependence in all aspects of life, including the environment and the economy.

8. Open-ended: The curriculum is open-ended in two ways: It is open to revision and continued refinement, and it provides open access to all students so that students are not tracked into dead-end careers.

9. Outcomes based: The curriculum focuses on outcomes so that students develop the critical skills and acquire the knowledge they need for effective lifelong learning and full functioning as citizens in a changing society.

---

presently exist, the principal can lead the faculty in using either an inductive or deductive process.

In using either the inductive or the deductive process, leaders should check state standards as a source of educational goals. Usually, a group of subject standards can suggest a goal.

Using the Inductive Process

In using the inductive process, the principal first identifies the educational programs that exist in the school. In most schools, three programs make a contribution: the activities program, the student services program, and the curriculum program. Schools that require students to participate in volunteer programs would add the volunteer program; those that have extensive apprenticeships or mentorships would include those as well.

The process begins by asking the faculty responsible for each of the noncurricular programs to identify their goals. Here, for example, is a goal for the activities program:

> Students will develop the skills and knowledge needed for effective leadership.

Even though most of these programs operate without explicit goals, the goal statement is useful in several ways: It provides a focus for faculty efforts; it provides a basis for evaluation; it provides a rationale for continuance.

The other part of the inductive process is for each subject matter team (or for special committees structured around the subjects) to identify the goals for that subject. Here is an example of a goal for science:

> Students will become competent in the field of science, developing an understanding of scientific concepts, acquiring scientific curiosity, valuing science as a way of knowing, and using knowledge to solve scientific problems.

Those separate goal statements are then combined and reviewed in their entirety by the faculty. The inductive process is based on the commonsense understanding that these programs exist, that they will continue to exist, and that they have implicit goals that need only be made explicit. The inductive process is simpler than the deductive one explained next; its chief limitation is that it may simply serve to maintain the status quo. It also runs the risk of ignoring important curriculum goals that transcend the traditional subjects, such as "develop learning skills."

Using the Deductive Process

In using the deductive process, the faculty members wipe the slate clean and take a completely fresh look at what they are trying to achieve. In most instances, they invite parents, older students, and other citizens to join them in the process. Usually the process follows this sequence.

1. The principal orients the group about the importance and nature of their task, emphasizing that they will identify the broad educational goals for the entire educational experience—all programs, all grades.

2. The principal helps the group develop the knowledge base, reviewing information such as the following: the changing nature of the society; the shape of the future; the nature of the community; the special characteristics of the student body; current research on curriculum, teaching, and learning.

3. The participants review goal statements developed by professional organizations (such as the Association for Supervision and Curriculum Development), by their own state and other states, and by other school systems. An excellent source of goal statements is Goodlad (1984). Even though a bit dated, the list developed by Goodlad seems to be a comprehensive one that could easily be modified for current use. The group should also find it helpful to review the state standards.

4. With the principal playing an active role, the participants decide on the general issues that will affect their work: Will the goal statement emphasize the subjects in the curriculum or transcend those subjects? How specific should the goal statement be? What format should be used?

5. With these matters resolved, each group develops its own tentative list of goals.

6. The several statements are synthesized into one comprehensive list that is reviewed, systematized, and organized so that it is clear, coherent, and nonredundant.

7. The final list is presented to the superintendent and then to the school board.

An example of a statement of goals produced by a middle school faculty is shown as Table 6.2.

Aligning Goals With Programs and Subjects

If the deductive process has been used, the educational goals need to be aligned with the school's educational programs; the curriculum goals then need to be assigned to the individual subjects.

TABLE 6.2 Central Middle School's Educational Goals for
Middle School Learners

Learning skills
Read with understanding and critical judgment.
Write clearly and effectively, and use writing as a way to learn.
Speak and listen well, especially in structured situations.
Use mathematical problem-solving processes.
Reason logically and think critically.
Study and learn effectively.
Use the computer to solve problems, compose, and process information.
Basic academic subjects
Learn important concepts and the special skills of:
    English language and literature
    Mathematics
    Science
    Foreign language
    Social studies
    The arts
Health and physical education
Understand the nature and importance of physical and mental health.
Develop physical fitness and recreation skills.
Creative thinking and expression
Learn how to express ideas and images creatively in a variety of media.
Learn how to think and to solve problems creatively.
Personal skills and attitudes
Develop a positive self-image.
Make sound moral decisions.
Develop special interests and leisure activities.
Cope with changes in family, community, and society.
Make sound decisions about careers, finances, use of media, and other
important personal issues.
Develop desirable attitudes toward work and study.
Develop motivation to learn.
Interpersonal skills and attitudes
Work cooperatively with others.
Value own ethnic identity and respect that of others.
Treat others with respect, regardless of age, gender, class, or ethnic
    origin.
Become a contributing member of the family.
Develop attitudes of responsible citizenship.
Develop an awareness of global interdependence.

TABLE 6.3 Analyzing Educational Goals

Directions: **For each educational goal listed, indicate which program should be** *primarily responsible* **by putting the letter** *R* **in the appropriate cell. Then indicate which other programs should** *contribute* **by using the letter** *C.*

	Curriculum Program	*Activity Program*	*Student Services Program*
Educational Goal			
1. Become a good citizen	R	C	
2. . . .			

NOTE: To conserve space, only one goal is shown here.

Once the comprehensive set of educational goals has been developed, a committee led by the principal first needs to allocate the educational goals to the programs offered in the school. A form similar to the one shown in Table 6.3 is useful here. Note that it lists across the top the three basic educational programs—the curriculum, the activities program, and the student services program (including guidance and health). The goals are listed down the left-hand side. The committee considers each goal to determine which program should be primarily responsible for, and which should contribute to, the accomplishment of that goal.

Once the general curriculum goals have been thus identified, they must be allocated to the several subjects. In this process, a matrix listing the curriculum goals down the left-hand side and the subjects across the top can be helpful. Respondents use the same symbols explained in Table 6.3 (*R* for *primarily responsible; C* for *contribute*). An example is shown in Table 6.4. Each teacher should complete the form, with a secretary compiling the results. The results are then discussed in a faculty meeting to ensure that each goal is emphasized in at least one subject and reinforced in others.

By means of these goal-related tasks, the faculty members working together have produced the following:

1. A list of broad educational goals for the entire educational program
2. A list of goals for the activity program, which can be used to give direction to that program

TABLE 6.4 Allocating Curriculum Goals to the Subjects

Directions: **For each of the curriculum goals listed below, indicate which subjects you think should be** *primarily responsible* **for that goal, using the symbol** *R.* **Then indicate which other subjects should** *contribute,* **using the symbol** *C.*

Curriculum Goals	Arts	English	Math	Science	Social Studies
1. Become a good citizen	C	C		C	R
2. ...					

NOTE: To conserve space, only one goal is shown here.

3. A list of goals for the student services program, providing guidance for that staff
4. A set of goals for each subject in the curriculum (can be used to both develop and evaluate the curriculum)

Throughout the process, the principal should emphasize its importance. It is not simply a rhetorical exercise; it results in meaningful goals that will be used to develop, evaluate, and improve the entire educational program. The processes explained in this chapter should result in documents that will be useful in the entire curriculum-making process, providing a foundation for all the curriculum work that follows.

References

Fullan, M. G. (1991). *The new meaning of educational change.* New York: Teachers College Press.
Goodlad, J. I. (1984). *A place called school.* New York: McGraw-Hill.
Moore, C. M. (1987). *Group techniques for idea building.* Newbury Park, CA: Sage.

7

Rethinking the
Program of Studies

The statements of the curriculum vision and goals can be very useful in the next important step, developing the school's program of studies. The program of studies is the total set of offerings provided for a group of learners at a particular level of schooling. In developing the program of studies, the principal and the faculty have essentially two choices: (a) *Renew* the program of studies by fine-tuning the existing program of studies to be sure that it is serving the present student body effectively, or (b) *restructure* the program of studies, reconceptualizing the entire curriculum as a completely new program of studies. Both processes are useful when one or more of the following conditions exist: (a) The school faces an accrediting review; (b) the student body seems to have changed significantly; (c) student achievement has not improved satisfactorily over the course of a few years; and (d) new leadership creates a climate for change. This chapter explains both the renewing and the restructuring processes.

Renewing an Existing Program of Studies

The principal and the faculty should consider renewing the existing program when they believe only minor changes are needed or when resources are limited. The following process has been used successfully by several schools:

1. *Develop the knowledge base.* Organize reliable information about the following: student demographics, student achievement, student success at the next level of schooling or in careers, cost of offering each subject, faculty loads, and class size. Also, review current research on curriculum, teaching, and learning.

2. *Identify the constraints and resources.* Check state requirements with respect to required subjects, grade levels, credits, and time allocations. Analyze the nature of the district's core curriculum. Assess the budgetary and other resources available.

3. *Determine the criteria to be used in evaluating the present program of studies.* The following criteria are suggested (see Glatthorn, 1994, for additional detail):

The program of studies is

1. Goal-oriented: focuses on goals and enables students to accomplish the district's mastery goals.
2. Balanced: provides an appropriate balance between required and elective subjects.
3. Integrated: emphasizes the interconnectedness of learning while giving appropriate emphasis to the subjects.
4. Skills reinforced: reinforces essential skills (such as writing and studying) across the curriculum.
5. Open-ended: does not track students into dead-end programs.
6. Responsive: responds to the special needs of learners.
7. Productive: achieves the results intended.

4. *Use the criteria in designing a comprehensive evaluation.* For each criterion, identify the methods that will be used in gathering data. Here are the methods that can be used:

- Survey: Parents, faculty, students
- Interview: Parents, faculty, students, administrators
- Observe: Classrooms, student activities, other areas
- Analyze documents: Test scores, vision and goal statements, other documents

5. *Systematize data, make final assessments for each criterion, and report results in a public document.* The final report should include the fol-

lowing elements: executive summary, methods used, evaluations for each criterion, recommendations for action.

6. *Discuss the final report with parents and teachers and prepare a strategy for action.* The strategy for action should include specific steps that will be taken to improve the program of studies. The following strategies might be undertaken:

- Add a new course.
- Drop an existing course.
- Modify existing courses.
- Combine two or more courses.
- Modify requirements and time allocations.
- Change the school schedule.
- Change instructional organization by creating new teams and modifying grouping arrangements.

Because all these changes have major implications for student learning, staffing, and budget, they should be reviewed by the faculty, discussed with parents and students, and presented to the school board for their review.

Restructuring the Program of Studies

As noted earlier, restructuring is a radical process of reconceptualizing and redesigning an entire program of studies for a given level of schooling. Such radical restructuring efforts typically attempt to accomplish two key redesign goals:

1. Redefine the nature of general education by specifying what all students should know, emphasizing outcomes, not courses and credits.
2. Rethink the way learning experiences should be organized to accomplish those outcomes by ignoring existing subject matter distinctions.

This section reviews current approaches to restructuring and then explains a process that schools can use.

Current Approaches

At the time of this writing, there seem to be several current approaches to restructuring programs of study:

1. Sizer's (1992) work with his Coalition of Essential Schools focuses on a smaller range of curricular goals in order to reduce class size and focus instruction.

2. Adler's (1984) Paideia Group is concerned chiefly with rethinking instructional processes. His work seems to be somewhat conservative, emphasizing the major disciplines.

3. Gardner's (1983) Multiple Intelligences approach uses the following multiple intelligences as redesign concepts: linguistic, musical, logical-mathematical, spatial, bodily-kinesthetic, interpersonal, intrapersonal (see Lazear, 1991, for practical applications).

4. Ways of Knowing emphasizes the essential ways of knowing (aesthetic, scientific, interpersonal, intuitive, narrative, formal, practical, and spiritual). Though there is as yet no systematic curriculum work being done here, the theory and concepts are well articulated in Eisner (1985).

5. The Comer (1988) model emphasizes the decision-making process, parent involvement, and the provision of comprehensive services to the disadvantaged; the curriculum is a comprehensive one, giving attention to the social, affective, and cognitive development of the child.

6. Success for All is designed to ensure success for all children in the beginning years of schooling. Its key features are the following: (a) a reading program that integrates whole language and phonics for 90 minutes each day, (b) homogeneous reading groups, (c) one-to-one tutoring, (d) cooperative learning, and (e) family support services (see Slavin & Yampolsky, 1992, for research on its effectiveness).

7. Accelerated Schools emphasizes three core principles: unity of purpose, school site empowerment, and building on strengths. The curriculum gives special attention to language in all subjects, providing an early introduction to writing and reading for meaning (see Levin, 1988).

8. The Copernican Plan (Carroll, 1994) is chiefly identified with block scheduling that provides extended periods of time (90 or more minutes) for the intensive study of fewer subjects. Carroll notes as well that such scheduling also includes evaluation based on mastery credit, individual learning plans, and the dejuvenalizing of high schools.

Each of these plans has its own advocates who report success with that program. One of the few systematic reviews of the effectiveness of such programs (including Comer, Paideia, Sizer, and Success for All) reached several conclusions: (a) Most of the programs studied had some research support; (b) these restructuring programs are feasible; (c) none can be made "teacher-proof"; and (d) Success for All seems to have the greatest externally developed research support (Herman & Stringfield, 1995).

Perhaps the best advice about choosing a total program is to check its "track record." Three sources are very helpful here: Slavin and Fashola (1998), Herman (1999), and James (1997). All three sources are objective, without bias toward any program, and results oriented, using student growth and achievement as the basic measures.

A "Homegrown" Process

Schools wishing to develop their own homegrown model of restructuring can use a process similar to the following:

1. As explained in the preceding chapter, identify the general educational goals and the outcomes to be achieved through all program components.

2. Review those educational goals and determine which are the goals of the mastery curriculum—that structured, planned part of the curriculum. These become the mastery curriculum goals—the outcomes to be achieved through the structured curriculum.

3. Identify the new organizing structures by which those mastery goals can be achieved. The organizing structures are the new "courses," although it might be better to think of them as the major concepts or themes by which learning is organized. Because this is a highly creative process, it is difficult to be formulaic about it. However, these are some approaches that can be used:

- Review the existing attempts listed earlier to see what can be learned from them.
- Reflect about the goals and try to find clusters and patterns that link them.
- Consider existing subjects. It may well be that the best way to understand mathematical concepts and skills is through a course called "mathematics." However, be alert to new ways by which those old courses might be linked—such as in a course called Technological Systems that would combine science, mathematics, and social studies.

• Consider the learners—their needs and interests.

In thinking about new structures, play with diagrams or schematics.

4. Through this brainstorming process, identify a small number (perhaps three to seven) organizing structures. List them and note the traditional subjects from which they will draw their content. Here is one example for middle school:

> *Problem solving* (math, science, social studies)
>
> *Wellness* (health, science, physical education, social studies)
>
> *Creative studies* (language arts, technology, science, home economics, music, art)
>
> *Community* (social studies, science, language arts)
>
> *Communication* (language arts, computer science, science, social studies, art)
>
> *Special interests* (a range of electives not restricted to subjects)

5. For each organizing structure, identify the model or models of teaching that would probably be most effective (see Joyce & Weil, 1991, for a full explication of the models).

6. Develop a matrix that shows the relationship between the mastery goals identified and the new structures to ensure that all goals have been emphasized, without excessive repetition. Make any modifications necessary.

7. Summarize the results in a large chart that shows the following: the organizing structure, the mastery goals it will be responsible for, the model of teaching it will emphasize, and the percentage of the total program time it will require.

8. Develop a sample weekly schedule showing the new organizing structures, the time allocated, and how they fit into a schedule. Consider using radical new scheduling approaches (such as that proposed by the Copernican plan). Developing the sample schedule is a practical test of the feasibility of the program.

9. Develop scope and sequence charts for the new organizing structures. For each organizing structure, identify its strands, the major recurring elements that will be emphasized in each grade level. For each strand and each grade, identify the major outcomes that students will achieve.

10. Use that scope and sequence as the basis for writing the new units of study.

Some Final Notes on Renewing or Restructuring

Both renewing and restructuring the program of studies have their own advantages. Renewing is simpler, takes less time, uses fewer resources, and is less risky for all involved. Restructuring is systemic, comprehensive, and bolder in conception. The principal and faculty need to give careful study to each approach before jumping on the current bandwagon.

References

Adler, M. J. (1984). *The Paideia program: An educational syllabus.* New York: Macmillan.

Carroll, J. M. (1994). The Copernican plan evaluated: The evolution of a revolution. *Phi Delta Kappan, 76,* 105-113.

Comer, J. P. (1988). Educating poor minority children. *Scientific American, 259,* 42-48.

Eisner, E. (Ed.). (1985). *Learning and teaching the ways of knowing.* Chicago: University of Chicago Press.

Gardner, H. (1983). *Frames of mind: The theory of multiple intelligences.* New York: Basic Books.

Glatthorn, A. A. (1994). *Developing the quality curriculum.* Alexandria, VA: Association for Supervision and Curriculum Development.

Herman, R. (1999). *An educators' guide to school wide reform.* Washington, DC: American Institute for Research.

Herman, R., & Stringfield, S. (1995, April). *Ten promising programs for educating disadvantaged students: Evidence of impact.* Paper presented at the annual meeting of the American Educational Research Association, San Francisco.

James, D. W. (1997). *Some things do make a difference for youth.* Washington, DC: American Youth Policy Forum.

Joyce, B., & Weil, M. (1991). *Models of teaching* (4th ed.). Englewood Cliffs, NJ: Prentice Hall.

Lazear, D. (1991). *Seven ways of knowing: Teaching for multiple intelligences.* Palatine, IL: Skylight.

Levin, J. M. (1988). *Accelerated schools for at-risk students.* New Brunswick, NJ: Center for Policy Research in Education.

Sizer, T. R. (1992). *Horace's school: Redesigning the American high school.* New York: Houghton Mifflin.

Slavin, R. E., & Fashola, O. S. (1998). *Show me the evidence! Proven and promising programs for America's schools.* Thousand Oaks, CA: Corwin.

Slavin, R. E., & Yampolsky, R. (1992). *Success for All: Effects on students with limited English proficiency.* Arlington, VA: Educational Research Service.

8

Committing to a Learning-Centered Schedule

Although many professors of school administration seem to sneer at schedule making as only a minor "technical" skill, it is instead a crucial aspect of school effectiveness and plays an important role in delivering a quality curriculum. Essentially, the schedule can be seen as the mechanism by which resources are allocated—time, space, and personnel. In a sense, they who control the schedule control the school's resources. This chapter argues for a learning-centered schedule and explains how principals can make the school's schedule more facilitative of student learning and supportive of the curriculum.

The Nature of a Learning-Centered Schedule

To understand the goal of efforts in this area, it is important to know what constitutes a good schedule. The key attributes are listed in Table 8.1 and discussed below, first in general terms and then more specifically.

The first general observation to note about these attributes is that many of them contradict each other. For example, if the only consideration is to maximize learning time, teachers would have no planning time. If a teach-

TABLE 8.1 Characteristics of a Learning-Centered Schedule

---

1. The schedule maximizes instructional time. The schedule reflects curricular priorities and gives first priority to students' learning needs. Administrators and teachers cooperate in defending instructional time.

2. The schedule facilitates the professional growth of teachers so that they have time to plan collaboratively and to cooperate in fostering their professional growth.

3. The schedule reflects grouping practices that do not stigmatize students, give all students access to a quality curriculum, and foster student achievement.

4. The schedule gives teachers a teachable situation. Teachers are assigned to their area of specialization. Wherever possible, teacher preferences about the number and type of preparations and room assignments are given consideration. Classes are neither too large nor excessively heterogeneous.

5. The schedule is flexible and learning oriented. Time is organized according to learning needs, instead of learning being constrained by rigid time frameworks.

6. The schedule is responsive to the needs of students and teachers, allowing sufficient time for relaxing, eating, and taking care of personal needs.

SOURCES: Anderson (1985), Dempsey and Traverso (1983), and Glatthorn (1986).

able assignment reflecting teacher preferences is all that matters, many teachers would have homogeneous classes. These contradictions suggest that the schedule-making process is essentially a negotiation of trade-offs, which will give the best combination of several compromises.

The second point to make is that these attributes are operationalized in a somewhat differential manner, depending on school level and type of schedule. Elementary teachers in a self-contained classroom and middle school teachers with a block-of-time schedule can make many of these decisions on their own. High school teachers coping with a complex period schedule face more troublesome constraints.

In examining the specific issues identified in the table, the first and most important consideration is that the schedule maximizes instructional time and reflects curricular priorities. Noninstructional time such as study and homeroom periods is kept to a bare minimum. Elementary and middle school teachers allocate time to the several subjects on the basis of the school's curricular priorities, not their own preferences. This guideline is especially significant for elementary mathematics and science. The research in general suggests that many elementary teachers give relatively little time to those subjects because they feel poorly prepared to teach them.

Time allocations are important also within a subject, once the schedule has been set. Consider, for example, two fifth-grade teachers planning their language arts instruction. One gives a great deal of time to the study of formal grammar and slights the teaching of writing; the other gives no time to the teaching of formal grammar and increases the time given to the teaching of writing. The results their students achieve reflect the way the teachers have allocated time: The first class learns formal grammar, a rather useless body of knowledge; the second class learns to write, an essential means of communication.

Once those allocations have been made, administrators and teachers should cooperate in defending instructional time. They make an explicit contract with each other to keep to an absolute minimum intrusive behaviors, such as calling students from a class, shortening classes because of special assemblies, dismissing students early for extracurricular activities, and interrupting classes with messages and announcements. Though teachers often blame administrators for such practices, many teachers seem to operate on this principle: "No class intrusions—except when I want them."

The second characteristic is almost as important as the first. If teachers are to become truly professional as collaborative leaders, they will need increased time for planning and professional growth. As Little (1990) points out, in many schools the schedule is made without reference to teachers' professional growth needs and the school's need for collaborative planning for school improvement. A recent study of teachers' working conditions concluded that 64% of the teachers responding reported that they had less than one hour each day of preparation time or no time at all (Carnegie Foundation for the Advancement of Teaching, 1990). In the most effective schools, special time is provided so that teachers can plan collaboratively, implement peer coaching programs, undertake action research, and collaborate with the principal in school improvement programs.

Such special time is provided in several ways. Teacher aides and volunteers take over classes. Classes are combined for special assembly programs. The principal and the assistant principal substitute for teachers. And from time to time, half-day substitutes are used to provide longer periods of time for staff development and collaborative planning. Obviously, all these are compromises that take teachers away from their students, but the payoff seems to be worth the sacrifices.

The way students are grouped for learning is also a critical matter. Because the issue has been so often oversimplified and distorted, it would make sense to clarify three related terms before recommending solutions.

Tracking is assigning students to a stratified sequence of courses, with a particular post-high school focus, such as *general* or *vocational* or *college preparatory*. *Between-class grouping* is assigning students to a particular class on the basis of the student's achievement in that subject. Thus, a school might have three levels of mathematics, ranked by ability in mathematics.

Within-class grouping is a process by which a teacher groups students within a class for certain instructional purposes. For example, most elementary teachers divide their classes into three reading groups.

Although many educators are inclined to make the sweeping generalization that "ability grouping is completely wrong," a closer look at the research and the realities of teaching suggest the issue is more complex than it seems. Table 8.2 presents a summary of that research.

School systems that are trying to find the best answer to a very complicated problem have arrived at several compromise solutions. First, they minimize tracking at the high school, providing only two tracks: academic and tech-prep. The tech-prep program emphasizes a high-quality program in the core subjects along with technical education for students who aspire to such careers. Second, they provide an accelerated curriculum for the most gifted, who are grouped for special instruction. They use heterogeneous grouping as a basis for assigning students to classes but attempt to reduce the range of abilities in any given class.

This set of decisions should not be seen as the best answer to this complex problem. It suggests, instead, that faculties need to study the problem very carefully and work out a solution that results in better achievement without stigmatizing students who are deficient in verbal or mathematical abilities.

Teachers also need a teachable situation. A teachable situation includes the following elements: Class size is manageable; the ability range is not too extreme; teachers are teaching in the area for which they have prepared; teachers have access to good facilities, materials, and equipment; and students are not disruptive. The data suggest that the profession is far from achieving that desired state. Here are some selected findings from a study by the Carnegie Foundation for the Advancement of Teaching (1990):

- Teachers who report that they are assigned to teach subjects for which they are unqualified: 18%
- Teachers who say general support services for teaching are only fair or poor: 59%
- Teachers who report that they spend their own money for supplies and materials: 96% (On the average, they report spending $250 each term.)

TABLE 8.2 Summary of the Research on Ability Grouping

1. Curriculum tracking has several serious weaknesses. It results in the stratification of the student body on the basis of social class. It often results in the delivery of an impoverished curriculum to low-ability tracks. In most tracking systems, there is little student mobility (Oakes, 1985).

2. Ability grouping for the gifted seems effective, especially if it results in an accelerated curriculum (Rogers, 1991).

3. In a classroom in which competition is emphasized, the presence of students perceived as having low ability is a source of motivation for high-ability students; the presence of high-ability students decreases motivation for low-ability students (Nicholls, 1979).

4. Classes of extreme heterogeneity pose special problems for teachers; such classes are often more difficult for the teacher to manage and to individualize instruction (Evertson & Hickman, 1981).

5. In general, heterogeneous between-class grouping seems to achieve better cognitive and affective results for most students (Slavin, 1989).

6. Within-class grouping seems most effective in teaching mathematics. However, in teaching beginning reading, some form of the Joplin plan (where students are reassigned on the basis of reading ability) seems most effective (Slavin, 1989).

- Teachers who report that their classes are too large: 38%
- Teachers who report that they feel their office space is fair, poor, or not available: 75%
- Teachers who report that disruptive student behavior is a serious or somewhat serious problem in their school: 86%

Obviously many of these conditions result from starved school district budgets—a situation that is not easily changed. However, principals should continue to lobby professionally for increased funding.

The fifth guideline involves the flexible use of time. The best schedules serve the requirements of the teaching/learning transaction. Unfortunately, in most schools, learning is controlled by the schedule. In this sense, the elementary teacher in the self-contained classroom has the most desirable schedule. Teams of middle school teachers who are assigned a block of time that they can use flexibly also have this advantage. It is high school teachers who suffer the most here. If educators wanted to devise the worst possible schedule for learning, they probably would propose the standard high school schedule: 45 minutes a day for all subjects, with an occasional double period.

The difficulties of teaching in a rigid 45-minute schedule led the Commission on Restructuring the American High School to recommend strongly that high schools should develop more flexible schedules (Dyer, 1996).

Dissatisfaction with the status quo has led many high schools to experiment with flexible arrangements, such as the following: modular schedules (in which the schedule is built on short time increments, such as 15-minute modules); block-of-time schedules (in which a team of teachers is assigned a long block of time to divide as they see fit); rotating period schedules (in which a class that meets first period on Monday would meet second period on Tuesday, and so on); and the 6-day cycle (in which the schedule is rotated every 6th day, instead of on a weekly basis). The Dempsey and Traverso (1983) handbook is an excellent resource for more information about scheduling alternatives.

Whereas such schedules may seem only to tinker with the standard schedule, a more radical approach has been offered in the Copernican Plan, devised by Carroll (1990). The Copernican Plan provides for long blocks of time for intensive study. In one version of the plan, a student would study only two subjects at a time—one in the morning and one in the afternoon—for a 12-week period. Although the plan was initiated with great fanfare in the district where Carroll served as superintendent, full implementation of the plan was impeded by lack of board support. He summarizes the evidence supporting the effectiveness of this plan in his 1994 article.

Current modifications of the Copernican Plan use such varied terms as *block of time, extended period, 90-minute* schedules. Although equaling traditional schedules in facilitating student learning, they have several other advantages. They reduce the number of preparations for teachers; they provide extended time for teacher development and team planning. And they enable students to concentrate on a few subjects at a time.

However, several drawbacks can be noted. Anecdotal reports by several principals indicate that many teachers are not taking advantage of the extended period. Their pattern is this: teacher talk for 45 minutes; seat work for 45. Also, the complaints of teachers who believe students need to learn the subject over a 10-month sweep (such as world languages) have led principals to make several variations in the standard block of time.

The final guideline is a commonsense reminder that students and teachers are ordinary human beings who need time to relax, eat, and take care of personal needs. In the desire to increase instructional time, some schools have unwisely ignored these needs by reducing the length of the lunch period, cutting back on recess time, and requiring teachers to give up their planning period in order to "cover" for a teacher who has to leave early.

Developing a Learning-Centered Schedule

How can the principal and faculty work toward a schedule that is more learning centered? The first part of this section examines what they can do together and then what teachers with principal leadership can accomplish on their own.

Collective Action for Learning-Centered Schedules

The first need is for an organizational structure for accomplishing the goals of schedule revision—either an existing committee or a special task force. The first job of the committee or task force would be to identify the limits in which they have to work; such limits are typically set by the state and the local school board in specifying the minimum number of instructional hours for all schooling, the subjects to be offered, and, in many cases, the minimum number of hours for each subject.

The task force should then review the research cited here, as well as other sources they identify, to build their knowledge base. Ordinarily, it is wise to summarize the knowledge base in a two- or three-page handout that can be distributed to all teachers.

With those jobs accomplished, the task force should examine the following issues, usually in the order listed.

1. *How shall we organize the program of studies, grade by grade?* The *program of studies,* as explained in the previous chapter, is the total set of educational offerings for a given group of students. Answering this question necessitates resolving several specific issues such as (a) what subjects will be required, (b) which elective offerings will be made available, (c) how much curriculum integration will be provided, and (d) how much time will be allocated to each subject.

2. *How shall we assign students to this program of studies?* The central question here, of course, is whether students are assigned on a homogeneous or heterogeneous basis. The issue also involves determining whether a "mini-school," "alternative program," "school-within-a-school," or

other similar approaches will be used to divide larger schools into smaller units.

This issue also involves the vexing question of class size. Here it makes sense if teams of teachers throughout the school are given the responsibility of providing instruction for approximately the same number of students and are able to make their own decisions about class size and teacher load. For example, in some schools it has been possible to give one teacher in a large department or team a sharply reduced teaching schedule simply by increasing average class size by five or six.

3. *By what processes shall we staff for this program of studies?* This question involves matters such as whether teachers work together as teams, how teachers are assigned to subjects and groups of students, and how specialists (such as art, music, and physical education teachers) are used. In examining this issue, the committee should keep in mind the special needs of novice teachers. More than anyone else, they need a teachable situation to cope with the demands of the first year of teaching. In too many schools, teacher seniority dictates how teacher preferences are respected; thus, the beginners get the most difficult classes and the older hands get the easier assignments.

4. *What type of schedule can give the instructional staff the flexibility they need in maximizing learning?* It is at this stage that the task force should examine the scheduling alternatives described above, keeping in mind that the most complicated schedule is not necessarily the best one.

5. *How should time be allocated to the several subjects?* If the school system does not provide guidelines about this issue, the principal and the teachers should develop their own, ensuring that time allocations reflect curricular priorities. Elementary faculties may wish to consider these recommendations made by Goodlad (1984): reading and language arts, 1.5 hours each day; mathematics, 1 hour each day; social studies, 2.5 hours each week; science, 2.5 hours each week; health and physical education, 2.5 hours each week; arts, 3.5 hours each week. If teachers decide to integrate reading, language arts, and social studies, they should make the block of time reflect the individual allotments. Middle and high school teachers can consult other current sources that recommend for those levels.

6. *By what processes can space be allocated for maximum learning?* Space is always in short supply. And in too many instances, decisions about how space is allocated are made on the basis of power and seniority.

There is a need instead for professional deliberation about issues such as the following: What are the special space needs of the several subjects, and how can they best be accommodated? How can we allocate space so that "floating" is minimized? What space can we make available for teacher planning and other professional activities? How can the allocation of space foster collegial interaction?

7. *How can the personal needs of students and teachers and the professional needs of teachers be accommodated?* Here, the committee needs to be especially creative, particularly in finding ways to give teachers extended planning periods. One practical goal to aim for would be to provide every teacher with a single planning period on each of four days and two back-to-back planning periods on one day of the week. That double period would be set aside for team planning, with specific guidelines about its use.

Based on their study of these issues, the task force would make recommendations to the entire faculty for their further discussion and modifications.

How the Principal and Teachers Can Make More Effective Use of the Existing Schedule

Even if these major changes do not seem feasible in the school, there are still several ways that the principal and the teachers can make more effective use of an existing schedule.

First, the principal can work with teachers to help them allocate time within a particular subject so that it reflects priorities in that subject. One of the best ways to do that is for the teachers to develop yearly schedules that the principal can review. Chapter 12 explains this process.

With time allocations established for separate subjects and for components of a single subject, teachers need to examine—with the principal's help—how they use time in the classroom. As emphasized in several research reports, time on task is directly related to student achievement (see Walberg, 1995). Teachers should also be concerned with the *quality* of learning, not the *quantity*. Instead of being unduly concerned about "How much time on a task?" they should ask as well, "What is the quality of the task?"

To understand this matter, consider two classes: In Class A, the teacher seems almost obsessed with increasing time on task. He starts class promptly, takes care of business quickly, keeps youngsters busily engaged by close monitoring, makes smooth transitions, and ends just when the bell rings. However, throughout that high-task lesson, the students are working on drill-and-practice materials, emphasizing low-level comprehension of textbook knowledge.

Now in Class B, the teacher is more relaxed. He begins class with a few minutes of talk about last night's basketball game. He seems a bit slow in passing out materials. The transitions are a little rough. And he ends a few minutes early. But throughout the lesson, he has had the students engaged in high-quality learning: They are using knowledge to solve problems, working together cooperatively, and actively involved in communicating with each other.

Class B shows better quality learning. Here are some signs that indicate quality learning is taking place:

- The students are working hard, and the teacher is facilitating their learning by acting as a cognitive coach, providing the structure they need, modeling, giving cues. But students are doing most of the work.

- The students are solving problems, using what psychologists call *generative knowledge*—knowledge that is used and applied. They are minimizing *inert knowledge*—knowledge that lies fallow because it is not used.

- The students are asking questions. The teacher is stimulating their curiosity, prodding them to ask questions, and rewarding those who do so.

- The students are using language as a means of learning: They are talking in small groups, using writing as a means of learning. The teacher is encouraging and monitoring such use.

- The students are engaged in assessing their learning; they are evaluating their own work and the work of their classmates. The teacher is monitoring these student assessments and adding some, using the assessment process as a means of facilitating learning.

- Finally, and most important of all, the students are learning something significant. When they leave the classroom, they know more than when they entered—about something that matters. That is the crucial task. In assessing the teacher's performance, the observer and the teacher ask, "What did they learn this period that they didn't know when they walked in?"

Next, the principal and teachers can collaborate in defending instructional time. In too many schools, instructional time is reduced by actions such as making public address announcements, summoning students from class, and excusing students for special activities. Whereas teachers are wont to blame the principal, often the teachers who complain are the same ones who ask to have students excused. Defending instructional time also involves practices such as emphasizing promptness in reporting to class, reducing the incidence of class "cutting," improving student attendance, and reducing passing time between periods.

Finally, the principal and teachers can extend learning time in several ways. They can meet students before school. They can provide remediation after school. And they can give meaningful homework assignments for which students are held accountable.

Obviously the schedule has a major influence on what students learn. Although not directly affecting the content of that learning, a learning-centered schedule can support a quality curriculum.

References

Anderson, L. W. (1985). Policy implications of research on school time. *School Administrator, 40,* 25-28.

Carnegie Foundation for the Advancement of Teaching. (1990). *The condition of teaching: A state-by-state analysis, 1990.* Princeton, NJ: Author.

Carroll, J. M. (1990). The Copernican Plan: Restructuring the American high school. *Phi Delta Kappan, 71,* 358-365.

Carroll, J. M. (1994). The Copernican plan evaluated: The evolution of a revolution. *Phi Delta Kappan, 76,* 105-113.

Dempsey, R. A., & Traverso, H. P. (1983). *Scheduling the secondary school.* Reston, VA: National Association of Secondary School Principals.

Dyer, T. J. (1996). *Breaking ranks: Changing an American institution.* Reston, VA: National Association of Secondary School Principals.

Evertson, C. M., & Hickman, R. C. (1981). *The tasks of teaching classes of varied group composition.* Austin: University of Texas, Research and Development Center for Teacher Education.

Glatthorn, A. A. (1986). How does the school schedule affect the curriculum? In H. J. Walberg & J. W. Keefe (Eds.), *Rethinking reform: The principal's dilemma* (pp. 53-60). Reston, VA: National Association of Secondary School Principals.

Goodlad, J. I. (1984). *A place called school: Prospects for the future.* New York: McGraw-Hill.

Little, J. W. (1990). Conditions of professional development in secondary schools. In M. W. McLaughlin, J. E. Talbert, & N. Bascia (Eds.), *The contexts of teaching in secondary schools* (pp. 187-223). New York: Teachers College Press.

Nicholls, J. (1979). Quality and equality in intellectual development: The role of motivation in education. *American Psychologist, 34,* 1071-1084.

Oakes, J. (1985). *Keeping track: How schools structure inequality.* New Haven, CT: Yale University Press.

Rogers, K. B. (1991). *The relationship of grouping practices to the education of the gifted and talented learner.* Storrs: University of Connecticut, National Research Center on the Gifted and Talented.

Slavin, R. E. (1989). Grouping for instruction in the elementary school. In R. E. Slavin (Ed.), *School and classroom organization.* Hillsdale, NJ: Lawrence Erlbaum.

Walberg, H. J. (1995). Generic practices. In G. Cawelti (Ed.), *Handbook of research on improving student achievement* (pp. 7-20). Arlington, VA: Educational Research Service.

9

Integrating the Curriculum

Although there is currently much interest in curriculum integration, some concerns about too much integration have recently been raised. For that reason, it is recommended here that the school faculty, under the leadership of the principal, determine the nature and extent of integration. This chapter reviews the types of integration, discusses the arguments for and against curriculum integration, and suggests a constructive way of resolving the issue.

Types of Integration

Because the term *integrated curriculum* is used so loosely, it is probably wise with an examination of the types available (see Fogarty, 1991, for an alternative conceptualization).

Integrating While Retaining Separate Subjects

There are four ways to integrate the curriculum while maintaining the separate subjects.

1. *Correlation.* This term is used to ensure that the curricula of two related subjects (such as science and mathematics or social studies and English language arts) are developed so that their content supports each other. For example, students read colonial literature in English class while they are studying the colonial period in social studies.

2. *Skills across the curriculum.* The curriculum can be made more cohesive if developers ensure that skills such as reading, writing, and study skills are reinforced across the curriculum, not confined to English language arts.

3. *Unified curricula.* This term designates the design of the curriculum for a given subject so that the divisions of that subject are minimized and its holistic nature is stressed. Whole language and unified science are examples of unified curricula.

4. *Informal integration.* In this model, the teacher brings in content from one subject while emphasizing the skills and concepts of another. Thus, an elementary teacher teaching a social studies unit on Mexico would informally provide examples of Mexican art and music.

Integrating Two or More Subjects

Most of the current discussion of integration is concerned with the need to combine content from two or more different subjects, such as English language arts, social studies, and science. Three major approaches are often used here.

1. *Subject-focused integration.* In this model, the developers begin with one subject (such as social studies) and then combine content from related subjects (such as English language arts and the arts).

2. *Theme-focused.* In this model, developers begin by identifying major themes that would be of interest and consequence to students. They then choose content from any subject that can support the theme. For example, a unit on *Conflict and Violence* might include content from social studies, English language arts, science, and the arts.

3. *Project-focused.* In this model, developers identify a complex project that would involve the students, such as developing a model community. In the course of completing such a project, students would need to master skills and concepts from social studies, science, mathematics, the arts, and English language arts.

Other organizing structures can be found in the literature such as the following: world cultures (Understanding Central America), aesthetic principles (Form and Function in the Arts), minority cultures (The African American Experience), and eras of history (The Industrial Revolution).

Arguments Supporting Integration

Several arguments have been advanced supporting the practice of combining two or more separate subjects. First, the research generally supports this type of integration. Vars (1991) points out that more than 90 studies comparing integrated curricula with traditional curricula have concluded that students learn more with integrated approaches.

Several theoretical arguments are also advanced. Supporters point out that problems in the real world cannot be compartmentalized into one discipline. Solving a problem in water quality would require knowledge of science, mathematics, economics, and political science. They also note that student concerns (such as choosing a career) transcend the disciplines. Finally, they argue that preliminary research on the brain suggests that students learn better when learning is holistic, not fragmented. (See, for example, Caine & Caine, 1997.)

Arguments Questioning the Use of Integration

Not all curriculum experts are convinced that integration is totally desirable. Gardner and Boix-Mansilla (1994) are persuasive in arguing for the importance of disciplinary knowledge, noting that students' access to disciplinary knowledge is essential in acquiring a quality education. Their position is supported by Roth's (1994) experience in working with teachers to develop an integrated unit. She concluded that the thematic unit on "1492" resulted in very superficial knowledge on the part of students. Other advocates of subject-focused curricula, such as Bruner (1960), note that each discipline has its own way of knowing, its own standards for validating knowledge, and its own key concepts. And Brophy and Alleman

(1991) caution that many of the integrated units they have examined were poorly designed collections of activities, only loosely connected.

A Process for Resolving the Issue

Given the current state of knowledge about curriculum integration, it seems wise for a principal to work with the faculty in deciding how and to what extent they will want to integrate their curriculum. The following steps are recommended.

1. Appoint a curriculum integration task force, or use an existing structure. The essential function of the task force is to develop the school-based model. The group should include the principal, teacher representatives from each teaching team (either grade level or departmental), and a representative of central office staff. The task force would then take all the steps enumerated below.

2. Build the knowledge base: the research on integration, the research on effective teaching, and the availability of exemplary curriculum materials.

3. Analyze the district curriculum guides to determine to what extent integration seems feasible.

4. Analyze teachers' experience in developing and using integrated curricula, paying special attention to both successes and problems.

5. Examine carefully students' learning needs and community attitudes toward educational innovation.

6. Assess the resources available—especially time, learning materials, and expertise.

7. Study the recommendations offered in Table 9.1. They have been drawn from an analysis of the research and my own experience. Though they are based on a solid foundation of knowledge, they should be reviewed carefully for their application to the local context. Note that the recommendations are differentiated according to school level. At the elementary level, teaching the basic skills is the primary responsibility. At the high school level, the individual subjects have greater importance to stu-

TABLE 9.1 Recommendations for Curriculum Integration

Elementary schools

Give primary emphasis to the mastery of the basic skills of reading, writing, and mathematics.

For the curriculum in beginning reading, use a whole language approach, supplemented by structured teaching of phonics (see Juel, 1991, for the research on this issue).

For the curriculum in beginning mathematics, focus on that subject but show its applications in science.

For the science curriculum, focus on scientific understandings but show their application to and relationships with social studies content.

For the social studies curriculum, encourage the integration of content from the arts.

In all subjects that are highly verbal in nature, develop curriculum materials that will facilitate the learning of reading, writing, and study skills.

Middle schools

Give primary emphasis to the study of issues and problems that have developmental significance for middle school learners.

Continue the emphasis on reading, writing, and study skills in the content areas.

Develop integrated units that combine English language arts, the arts, and social studies in helping middle school learners deal with issues that are developmentally significant.

Develop integrated units in science, technology, and health that will provide students with a sound knowledge base in making major behavioral choices.

Structure the mathematics curriculum so that it continues to emphasize mathematical concepts and skills, while showing the applications of mathematics to students' daily lives.

Ensure that science and mathematics are closely correlated so that students have mastered the mathematical skills required for science.

High schools

Give primary emphasis to the mastery of the key concepts and skills of each discipline.

Continue the emphasis on reading, writing, and study skills across the curriculum.

Ensure close correlation of advanced sciences and mathematics.

Develop an *American Studies* course that carefully integrates American literature, American history, and the arts.

---

dents facing career and college demands. At the middle school level, freed from the pressure to both teach the basics and emphasize the subjects, the faculty have much greater freedom to innovate.

8. Develop the school's model of integration. To encourage a sense of ownership, emphasize the importance of a "grassroots" approach that represents teachers' recommendations.

With the school's model selected, each teaching team collaborates in developing the first unit. They implement the unit and evaluate its effectiveness, reporting the results to the task force.

After analyzing the team reports, the task force should modify the model if necessary and develop a long-term calendar for planning and teaching the next five units.

This cyclical process of planning, teaching, evaluating, and revising is likely to result in high-quality units.

References

Brophy, J., & Alleman, J. (1991). A caveat: Curriculum integration isn't always a good idea. *Educational Leadership, 49*(2), 66.

Bruner, J. (1960). *The process of education.* Cambridge, MA: Harvard University Press.

Caine, R. N., & Caine, G. (1997). *Education on the edge of possibility.* Alexandria, VA: Association for Supervision and Curriculum Development.

Fogarty, R. (1991). Ten ways to integrate curriculum. *Educational Leadership, 49* (2), *61-65.*

Gardner, H., & Boix-Mansilla, V. (1994). Teaching for understanding in the disciplines—and beyond. *Teachers College Record, 96,* 198-218.

Juel, C. (1991). Beginning reading. In R. Barr, M. L. Kamil, P. B. Mosenthal, & P. D. Pearson (Eds.), *Handbook of reading research, Vol. 2* (pp. 759-788). New York: Longman.

Roth, K. J. (1994). Second thoughts about interdisciplinary studies. *American Educator, 18*(1), 44-47.

Vars, G. F. (1991). Integrated curriculum in historical perspective. *Educational Leadership, 49*(2), 14-15.

10

❦

Aligning the Curriculum

Several different types of curriculum are at work in the school. When they are reasonably congruent with each other, student achievement is improved. This chapter reviews briefly the several types of curriculum and then explains how a comprehensive model for aligning these curricula can be planned and executed.

Types of Curricula

Seven types of curricula need the attention of the principal.

- *Recommended curriculum.* The *recommended* curriculum is that which is recommended by scholars and professional organizations. The best source for the recommendations of professional organizations is Kendall and Marzano (1997).
- *Written curriculum.* The *written* curriculum, as the term is used here, is the curriculum that appears in state and locally produced documents, such as state standards, district scope and sequence charts, district curriculum guides, teachers' planning documents, and curriculum units.

- *Taught curriculum.* The *taught* curriculum is that which teachers actually deliver day by day.

- *Supported curriculum.* The *supported* curriculum includes those resources that support the curriculum—textbooks, software, and other media.

- *Assessed curriculum.* The *assessed* curriculum is that which appears in tests and performance measures: state tests, standardized tests, district tests, and teacher-made tests.

- *Learned curriculum.* The *learned* curriculum is the bottom-line curriculum—the curriculum that students actually learn.

- *Hidden curriculum.* This is the unintended curriculum. It defines what students learn from the physical environment, the policies, and the procedures of the school. Here is an example. Each week teachers in an elementary school devote 250 minutes to reading and 50 minutes to art. Students learn this lesson: "In this school, art is not considered very important."

Figure 10.1 shows the relationship of these curricula as they interact with each other. Notice that the research suggests there are varying patterns of influence among the several types. The recommended curriculum seems to have little influence on the written, although districts seem to be increasingly concerned with state standards, especially if they are accompanied by state tests. Also, the standards developed by the National Council of Teachers of Mathematics (1989) seem to have had a significant influence in the development of district mathematics guides.

The written curriculum seems to have a moderate influence on the taught curriculum. Teachers report that they typically check the district guide early in the year, just to remind themselves what it includes. They are much more influenced by the assessed curriculum, especially if they are held accountable for students' results. Students are similarly sensitive to the assessed curriculum, as evidenced in the standard student question, "Is this going to be on the test?"

Teachers are perhaps most sensitive to the learned curriculum, making their decisions on the basis of students' needs, as they perceive them, and students' responses to the taught curriculum. Whereas conventional wisdom holds that teachers are textbook driven, the research suggests that the textbook is only one of several sources that the teacher consults in planning for instruction (see Brown, 1988).

And textbook series often do not match closely the written curriculum because they are developed for a nationwide mass market. A relationship often exists between the written and the assessed curricula. Typically, the assessment is an objective test that samples low-level learning.

Figure 10.1 Types of Curricula

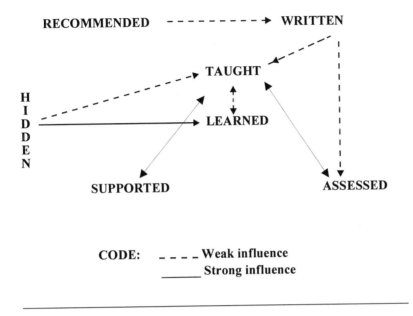

CODE: _ _ _ _ Weak influence
                        Strong influence

The hidden curriculum has a strong influence on what students learn. Even though students are not always aware of the impact of the hidden curriculum, they experience it every day. For example, an old building with holes in the roof and graffiti on the walls very clearly conveys the message, "People here don't care about this school."

These gaps have led experts in the field to recommend alignment processes.

English (1992), the chief advocate of alignment, emphasizes the need for a close match between the curriculum and the test. He explains that alignment can be achieved through "frontloading" or "backloading." Frontloading means developing the curriculum first and then finding a test to match; backloading means developing (or locating) the test first and then developing a curriculum to match.

I recommend a more comprehensive approach that involves the alignment of all seven curricula. The alignment process is best carried out at the school level. Even though a district or regional approach might be more efficient, the school-based process results in a greater sense of ownership and serves to educate the teachers about the details of the new curriculum guide.

Aligning the Recommended
and the Written Curricula

Aligning the recommended and the written curricula is primarily the responsibility of the task force assigned to develop the curriculum in a given subject area. However, the principal can play a role, as explained below.

The extent to which the recommended curriculum should determine the written curriculum varies from subject to subject. Some professional standards, such as those in mathematics, seem to be well formulated and widely approved; they thus can provide a useful guide for the written curriculum. On the other hand, the standards for English language arts (National Council of Teachers of English and International Reading Association, 1996) have been widely criticized for being too vague and excessively concerned with process; they therefore seem less useful to local developers.

Principals can play an active role in this alignment. If they are members of task forces, they can require the task force to analyze professional and state standards and determine which ones should be used in the district guide. If they are not represented on the task force, they can examine the products to assess whether the recommended curriculum has been given sufficient attention.

Aligning the Written,
the Supported, and the Assessed Curricula

The principal should play an active role in working with teachers to align the written, the supported, and the assessed curricula. Because these three types are closely related, the alignment can be accomplished in one project. The following process has worked well with several school systems.

1. *Plan the project.* Appoint a curriculum alignment committee (or use an existing committee) to oversee and coordinate the project. Train the committee in the alignment process as it involves these three types of curriculum. The alignment committee should then train the grade-level teams, who will carry out the alignment tasks for their grade.

2. *Focus the curriculum.* The grade-level teams should carefully analyze the new district curriculum to focus the alignment process on the *mastery objectives.* As the term is used here, the mastery objectives are those that meet one or more of the following criteria:

- Will likely be tested or assessed
- Require explicit teaching

- Are best learned when they are carefully planned
- Are essential for all students to master

These mastery objectives are different from what I have termed *continuing development objects,* those outcomes that should be nurtured on every suitable occasion, not taught in a specific grade level. Here is an example to show the difference:

- *Mastery:* Define *metaphor.*
- *Continuing development:* Enjoy poetry.

Mastery objectives should be aligned with tests and texts; organic outcomes need not be.

The complete set of mastery objectives should be stored in a computerized database, organized by grade level and then by areas within that subject.

3. *Check to be sure that the district curriculum embodies the state standards.* The state standards will surely be reflected in state tests; they also provide useful guidelines for local developers.

4. *Analyze the tests.* Using a printout of the mastery objectives for their grade level, the teams should then indicate on an appropriate form which of the mastery objectives are likely to be tested. An example of the form that can be used in this process is shown in Table 10.1. In determining which of the mastery objectives are likely to be tested, the team should analyze state tests, district tests, and standardized tests. They need not analyze teacher-made tests because the assumption is that teachers will test what they have taught. In analyzing those tests, the team can use descriptions of test content and tests previously given and no longer considered confidential.

5. *Analyze the texts.* The final step is to determine where the mastery objectives are explained in the text. The team should check the table of contents and the index of the texts used, noting the page numbers where the topic is treated. The team should enter page numbers only if the topic is treated in sufficient depth. Textbooks often treat topics so superficially that the text is of little value to teachers and students.

6. *Evaluate the results.* The alignment committee should review all the work of the teams, noting any problems that need correcting and pro-

TABLE 10.1 Alignment Form

Subject: English language arts		Grade: 9
Mastery Objectives	*Tested*	*Text: English 9*
Define, identify metaphor	x	pp. 123-126
Listen critically		
Write personal narrative	x	pp. 16-17
Hold interview		p. 14

ducing a complete set for the entire school. This complete set will be useful for the principal and supervisors.

7. *Use the results.* Simply completing the alignment charts has little value. The results should be used to accomplish two tasks. First, as noted briefly below and explained more fully in Chapters 12 and 13, teachers should use the list of mastery objectives to develop yearly and unit plans that ensure adequate treatment of all the mastery objectives. Mastery objectives that are tested should receive the highest priority in planning for learning; continuing development objectives likely to be tested would have a second priority. Second, the team should institute plans to fill in the gaps in the textbook. They can order supplementary materials or write their own materials.

Aligning the Written and the Taught Curricula

The alignment charts described above can be very useful in aligning the written and the taught. Next to aligning the taught and the learned, this is probably the most important alignment of all. Even the most conscientious teachers will need help in ensuring that they are effectively delivering the written curriculum. As explained more fully in Chapters 12 and 13, the principal should help teachers develop yearly calendars and unit plans. In developing such plans, the teacher should systematically check off the mastery objectives as they are scheduled in the yearly calendar and included in the unit. When the principal reviews these plans, he or she should check to ensure that all mastery objectives are in fact included.

Aligning the Hidden and the Learned Curricula

Because the hidden curriculum has such an impact on student learning, it deserves special study by the principal and teachers. The principal may therefore wish to lead a special task force to make a systematic analysis. Here are the main factors that seem to constitute the hidden curriculum:

- *Time allocation.* For example, are health and physical education allocated sufficient time to change the behavior of children and youth?
- *Space allocation.* How much space is allocated for teacher conferring and planning?
- *Use of discretionary funds.* Who decides? How are such funds expended?
- *Student discipline.* Do suspensions seem to reflect an ethnic bias?
- *Physical appearance.* Does the appearance of facilities suggest that those in the building care for the school? Are walls decorated with student artwork?
- *Student activities program.* Does this program reflect and respond to student talent diversity?
- *Communication.* Are most of the messages over the public address system of a positive nature? How often are student voices heard?
- *Power.* Do teachers have power in the decision-making process? Do students have any real power over the factors that matter?

When the analysis of the hidden curriculum has been completed, the principal and the teachers should identify those hidden messages that do not reflect what they want students to learn—and then work together to alter discrepant elements. For example, if the principal and teachers believe in the importance of students' artistic creativity but discover that the hidden curriculum reveals no traces of creativity, they might want to change the hidden curriculum by decorating the corridors with student artwork.

Aligning the Taught and the Learned Curricula

The final and perhaps most important type of alignment involves the taught and the learned curriculum. Whereas teachers mistakenly assume that students learn all that they are taught, the evidence is otherwise. As Doyle (1986) points out in his review of the research, for much of classroom time students are either obviously off-task or feigning on-task behavior, only dimly aware of what the teacher is trying to teach.

This issue is so important that the principal and the teachers should discuss it in a faculty meeting or special workshop that would answer four questions: What is the taught/learned gap, and why is it important? What student factors cause it? What can teachers do to reduce the gap? What next steps should we take?

Nature and Importance of the Gap

The session should begin with an open dialog about the gap at their school. A simple definition should be helpful: "Students do not learn all that teachers teach. We call that the taught/learned gap." A brief discussion of its importance can follow.

Student Factors

The next part of the discussion is to examine the student factors that cause the taught/learned gap. Both the research and this author's experience indicate that the following elements are crucial.

First, students have limited attention spans. They have other agendas. The teacher may be doing his or her best to teach the parts of the amoeba, but student minds are on the weekend activities. All that television watching has conditioned them to expect one-minute messages. The physical environment may cause inattention. If the room is too warm, students will find it difficult to focus on a complex task.

Students may also lack knowledge and cognitive development. They are doing the best they can, but what they are hearing does not make sense. The terms are too difficult; the new knowledge is overwhelming. Students also may have special needs that are not being addressed. Even though they may not have obvious disabilities, they may have learning problems that interfere with their learning.

Peer pressure may also interfere with the learning process. This factor has a negative impact especially on economically disadvantaged minority students. They may want to learn, but a few powerful peers can establish norms that devalue learning.

Teacher-Facilitating Factors

In an atmosphere of inquiry, with teachers discussing their experience, the faculty should next analyze what seems to work. This discussion should have a positive tone so that teachers do not feel they are being blamed. These productive factors are the ones that will probably be identified:

1. Clarify the objective.
2. Help students find meaning and purpose in learning the objective.
3. Encourage students to ask questions.
4. Use learning strategies that require a high level of student activity.
5. Use frequent quizzing to monitor learning and maintain high alertness.
6. Observe for verbal and nonverbal signs of off-task behavior.
7. Use monitoring data to adjust instruction.

The workshop should end with a discussion of what can be done to determine how much of a gap exists and what can be done to reduce it. The following process should be useful.

1. Teachers pair off or work in collegial teams.
2. Teacher A plans a lesson with the help of Teacher B; they also prepare a comprehensive quiz based on that lesson.
3. Teacher A implements the lesson, while Teacher B observes both student and teacher behavior.
4. Teacher A administers the quiz at the end of the lesson.
5. They meet to discuss the results.
6. They then switch roles.

References

Brown, D. S. (1988). Twelve middle-school teachers' planning. *Elementary School Journal,* *89,* 69-87.

Doyle, W. (1986). Classroom organization and management. In M. C. Wittrock (Ed.), *Handbook of research on teaching* (3rd ed., pp. 392-431). New York: Macmillan.

English, F. W. (1992). *Deciding what to teach and test: Developing, aligning, and auditing the curriculum.* Newbury Park, CA: Corwin.

Kendall, J. S., & Marzano, R. J. (1997). *Content knowledge* (2nd ed.). Aurora, CO: Midcontinent Regional Educational Laboratory.

National Council of Teachers of English and International Reading Association. (1996). *Standards for the English language arts.* Urbana, IL: National Council of Teachers of English.

National Council of Teachers of Mathematics. (1989). *Curriculum and evaluation standards for school mathematics.* Reston, VA: Author.

11

Monitoring the Implementation Process

T he monitoring of the curriculum involves the use of processes to determine to what extent the approved curriculum has been implemented. This chapter reviews the argument about monitoring and then presents a model that maintains the advantages of monitoring while avoiding its drawbacks. The model can be used both as a basis for monitoring and as a guide for helping teachers implement the curriculum.

The Argument About Monitoring

Monitoring the implementation of curriculum is one of those issues that seem to be highly controversial and divisive. On the one hand, there are many policymakers and administrators who seem to distrust teachers, spending much time developing and implementing elaborate teacher-accountability systems. On the other hand, there are experts in the field who seem to believe that there should be no monitoring, with each teacher developing his or her own curriculum. Therefore, a review of the reasons advanced by each camp seems in order.

Reasons for Monitoring

Why should principals monitor the curriculum? Several reasons have been advanced. The first is simply one of efficiency: The district has spent a great deal of time and money in developing the curriculum. It would be a manifest waste of time if teachers simply ignored it. The second is one of consistent development. If the district curriculum has been carefully sequenced and articulated, monitoring will help ensure that what students are being taught in fourth grade builds on third and leads into fifth. Also, monitoring keeps the teachers alert and on task. If they know that their choice of curriculum content is being monitored, they will more likely select appropriate content from the guide. Finally, from the principal's perspective, monitoring is a useful process for helping the principal become more visible and involved with curriculum, one of the central components of school improvement.

There is some research support for these claims (see Cotton, 1995). Without monitoring, and left to their own devices, teachers will emphasize what they know best, without being overly concerned with the district curriculum. Elementary teachers will slight science and emphasize reading, if they are not monitored. Also, the research is clear that a carefully articulated curriculum leads to improved achievement, especially in mathematics in which grade-to-grade coordination is so crucial (Corbett & Wilson, 1992).

Reasons for Not Monitoring

Those who oppose monitoring also advance several persuasive reasons. First, they are concerned that very close monitoring implies distrust of teachers and therefore damages the school climate by placing administrators and teachers in adversarial roles. Second, insisting that the standard curriculum be faithfully implemented for all students ignores the reality of student and school differences. Many of those systems currently take the form of complex instructional management and accountability systems that have several features in common. Also, close monitoring with a concomitant emphasis on test scores forces the teacher to focus on testlike items, thus narrowing the curriculum and overemphasizing direct instruction. Finally, excessive monitoring reduces the teacher to a mechanical implementer of what others have produced, thus deskilling teaching.

Here again there is some evidence to support these claims. Miller's (1996) study of the Kentucky state accountability system (which emphasized close monitoring and teacher accountability for test results) concluded that it has had no measurable impact on student achievement; it has, instead, driven a wedge between teachers, parents, and schools and undermined teachers' sense of efficacy. Also, McNeil's (1986) study confirmed some of the worst fears of opponents of monitoring: The emphasis on monitoring and test scores resulted in a classroom characterized by a focus on testable learning, drill and practice on testlike items, and excessive use of direct instruction.

A Practical Solution

Over several years of working with school districts and reviewing the research, I have developed a monitoring system that maintains the advantages while avoiding the drawbacks of monitoring.

Establishing the Antecedent Conditions

Monitoring efforts are more likely to succeed if certain antecedent conditions are present:

1. *Emphasize mutual accomplishment, not total fidelity.* Mutual accomplishment (first identified by Bird, 1986) is a type of implementation in which the developers of an innovation (the district curriculum workers) accomplish their central goal of changing the curriculum and the users of the innovation (classroom teachers) accomplish their goals of influencing the curriculum and maintaining control of the essential elements of classroom life. Mutual accomplishment is a win/win philosophy of curriculum implementation. Working for complete fidelity is a win/lose approach: Administrators win and teachers lose.

2. *Influence the development of a "teacher-friendly" and "change-simple" curriculum.* As explained throughout this work, a teacher-friendly curriculum is one with these features: (a) It specifically provides time and space for teacher enrichment; (b) it is presented in a form that makes it easily accessible; and (c) it does not mandate a sequence or teaching approach. A change-simple curriculum is one that reflects the characteristics that Fullan (1991) has found are important in bringing about effective change. First, the curriculum is clear: Terms are defined clearly, and objectives are specified unambiguously. Second, the curriculum avoids excessive complexity: It does not expect the teacher to use too many resources, use complicated technology, or keep too many elements in mind. Finally, the curriculum is one of high quality: Teachers respect it and wish to implement it.

3. *Establish a culture that values continuous improvement and collaboration.* This is perhaps the most crucial antecedent condition. The principal should take leadership in clarifying the concept of continuous improvement, of emphasizing its role in making the school better, in modeling that philosophy, and in rewarding teachers who manifest it. Teachers should understand that curriculum development is an ongoing process, not a single event.

Collaboration is the other critical element in the school's culture. The principal should establish the importance of working together in a cooperative manner, should establish conditions that support collaboration, should model collaboration, and should reward teachers who cooperate. As Griffin (1988) has pointed out, such an attitude is especially crucial in developing a supportive environment for curriculum change.

**Taking Effective Action to
Achieve Mutual Accomplishment**

Once those antecedent conditions have been established, principals can then take effective action to achieve mutual accomplishment:

1. *Ensure that resources are available in a timely manner.* Principals can help by putting pressure on district personnel to order new texts and other materials early enough to ensure that they will be on hand for teachers' use. Teachers often express great frustration when essential materials do not arrive on time.

2. *Provide ongoing staff development that is sensitive to teachers' stages of concern.* Though the district is primarily responsible for providing the basic staff development required by the new curriculum, the principal should also take the initiative in ensuring that teachers have time to meet together to exchange ideas, share strategies, and solve common problems. Here, the research on teachers' stages of concern should be useful (see Loucks-Horsley & Stiegelbauer, 1991). In the early stages of developing a curriculum, teachers simply want to be kept informed. Their concerns later shift to personal issues: How will the new curriculum affect me? Only in later stages will they ask questions about its impact on student learning.

3. *Help teachers translate the district guide into long-term plans.* As explained more fully in Chapters 12 and 13, yearly planning calendars and units of study enable the teachers to translate the district guide into planning documents that teachers can use as they plan for instruction. The dis-

trict guide by itself is not sufficient as a guide to such planning; this additional work is necessary. Once teachers have developed long-term and unit plans, the principal can confer with them in a climate of dialogue. These questions can be raised:

- Have all the mastery objectives been suitably emphasized?
- Do time allocations reflect curricular priorities?
- Is the sequence one that will likely lead to mastery?

4. *Make several informal observations.* As explained more fully in another work, informal observations are short drop-in visits to classrooms, lasting only 5 to 10 minutes (see Glatthorn, 1990). In this brief period of time, the principal can observe to what extent the district curriculum is being implemented or enriched. If three such informal observations indicate that the teacher is spending too much time on unrelated curriculum issues, the principal can inquire in a constructive manner about the teacher's rationale for seeming to deviate from the curriculum.

The informal observations should not be used to evaluate teachers. They are an effective monitoring strategy. They also serve as a means of giving the teacher merited and timely praise—or as a distant early warning system of problems that may need systematic attention.

5. *Cheer for the curriculum.* The principal can serve as a cheerleader for the new curriculum and remind teachers of the need for effective implementation.

6. *Analyze test scores with teachers.* Although teachers should not be held totally accountable for students' test results, they should cooperate with the principal in examining schoolwide and classroom-specific results with an analytical perspective. Such a perspective examines systematically the following issues:

- Was the test congruent with the curriculum?
- Were the texts and other instructional materials congruent with the curriculum?
- Was sufficient time devoted to the content included in the test?
- Were students motivated to master the curriculum and perform well on the test?
- Did parents provide a supportive learning environment at home and emphasize the importance of the tests?

- Did teachers use effective instructional approaches?
- Was the curriculum itself of high quality?
- Which groups of students performed below expectations? Do they need additional time, more varied materials, or diversified teaching/learning activities?

This analysis should be carried out in an atmosphere of problem solving, not blaming or scapegoating.

A Concluding Note

Any monitoring system that balances the need for district curriculum coordination with the teachers' need for a measure of autonomy can be effective if it is implemented in a climate that supports continuous improvement and collegiality. The system described above has worked effectively for many school systems and schools, but principals and teachers are strongly encouraged to develop their own model.

References

Bird, T. (1986). Mutual adaptation and mutual accomplishment: Images of change in a field experiment. In A. Lieberman (Ed.), *Re-thinking school improvement: Research, craft, and concept* (pp. 45-60). Alexandria, VA: Association for Supervision and Curriculum Development.

Corbett, H. D., & Wilson, B. L. (1992). The central office role in instructional improvement. *School Effectiveness and School Improvement, 3,* 45-68.

Cotton, K. (1995). *Effective schooling practices: A research synthesis, 1995 update.* Portland, OR: Northwest Regional Educational Laboratory.

Fullan, M. G. (1991). *The new meaning of educational change.* New York: Teachers College Press.

Glatthorn, A. A. (1990). *Supervisory leadership.* New York: HarperCollins.

Griffin, G. A. (1988). Leadership for curriculum improvement: The school administrator's role. In L. N. Tanner (Ed.), *Critical issues in curriculum* (pp. 244-266). Chicago: University of Chicago Press.

Loucks-Horsley, S., & Stiegelbauer, S. (1991). Using knowledge of change to guide staff development. In A. Lieberman & L. Miller (Eds.), *Staff development for education in the 90s* (2nd ed., pp. 45-60). New York: Teachers College Press.

McNeil, L. M. (1986). *Contradictions of control: School structure and school knowledge.* New York: Routledge & Kegan Paul.

Miller, E. (1996, January/February). Early reports from Kentucky on cash rewards for "successful" schools reveal many problems. *Harvard Education Letter, 12,* 1-3.

PART

IV

Working With Teachers

12

❦

Making Yearly
Planning Calendars

The district curriculum guide is only a foundation for teachers' planning. Effective principals know how to help teachers use the guide to develop yearly and unit plans. This chapter explains the nature of yearly plans, provides a rationale for their use, suggests one way of organizing for yearly planning, and then presents a process by which a faculty can collaborate in the development and review of such plans. Chapter 13 then explains how teachers can use the yearly plan as a basis for unit planning. (Those interested in a full discussion of how teachers actually plan should consult Clark & Peterson, 1986, and Schmidt, Porter, Floden, Freeman, & Schwille, 1987.)

The Nature of Yearly Plans
and a Rationale for Their Use

Yearly plans are documents, usually in calendar form, that show the units that the teacher will teach through the course of the year. They may also indicate significant events occurring in the school community that will affect teaching and learning and identify the mastery benchmarks to be emphasized. In those schools in which subjects are taught intensively for one term rather than for an entire year, the term plan is substituted for the yearly plan.

For several reasons, the yearly plan is a very useful document. It fosters collaborative planning by a grade-level or subject team, because it is recommended that teachers work together in producing the plan. It provides a foundation for the more detailed unit plans by translating the curriculum guide into a series of units. It facilitates coordination across subject lines; as explained more fully later, it provides a simple means for examining the flow of instruction in two or more related subjects. It operationalizes the school's decisions with respect to curriculum integration. It shows the sequence of units across the year. And it shows clearly the time allocations teachers have made for the several units, thus providing a useful tool for curriculum monitoring.

Though the yearly plan has several reasons for recommending it, not all teachers are enthusiastic about developing and using yearly plans. Some see it as simply one more administrative requirement. Others complain that school life is so unpredictable that no plan can ever be an accurate portrayal of the actual teaching and learning that go on in the classroom. Given such teacher opposition, the principal needs to lay the groundwork, as explained below.

Organizing for Yearly Planning

Each school will use its own system for accomplishing the planning process. The procedures explained below have worked well with several schools.

Develop the Proposal

The first phase is to develop the school's proposal for yearly planning. The principal should introduce the concept of yearly planning during the spring semester, so that decisions can be made in a timely manner. In a faculty meeting devoted just to this topic, the principal (or one of the teacher-leaders) should make a 15-minute presentation on the concept of, and rationale for, yearly planning. Following that presentation, the teachers should meet in small groups to discuss their views and their present practice with respect to yearly planning, reporting the results of the group discussion to the entire faculty. If there seems to be general support for the process, the principal can then move into the next phase. If there is strong opposition, this should indicate that further study is needed. In this instance, the principal should take the time to explore more deeply the reasons for opposition and work with teachers to remove the obstacles that make them question the value of planning.

Once sufficient support has been developed, the principal should ask a special task force (or one of the existing school committees) to develop a specific proposal for faculty to examine. By reviewing this chapter, analyzing the literature, visiting schools using such plans, and sharing their own experience and knowledge, the task force should make a series of recommendations about the following issues (my own recommendations are explained more fully in the following sections):

- The format for yearly planning
- The contents of the yearly plan
- The structure by which they will be produced—team, department, or individual
- The review process
- The schedule for developing yearly plans

For each issue, a specific recommendation is made in the next section; however, it is important for the faculty to decide these matters. Once the proposal has been reviewed and revised, it should be adopted and disseminated as the school's process for yearly planning.

Though schools will vary in how they accomplish this initial organizing task, the principal should ensure that the school's planning structure and processes have been developed with significant teacher input.

Lay the Foundations

The next phase in the process is to establish the foundations for yearly planning.

1. *Develop the forms.* This is a crucial step, because the forms will also dictate content. Table 12.1 shows one form that has been used successfully with many schools; Table 12.2 shows a form that elementary teachers seem to prefer. The form in Table 12.1 includes four essential planning items. It first shows the weeks of the school year, in sequence. For each week, it notes any events that will affect teaching and learning, including the following: national and state holidays, parent meetings, student extracurricular activities, and report card and parent conference days. It then notes the title of the unit and indicates the related mastery benchmarks. Some schools prefer to add a column for the textbook pages that support the unit.

TABLE 12.1 Recommended Form for Yearly Planning

Team: English II   Date submitted: 9/23

Weeks of Year	*Important Events*	*Unit Title*	*Mastery Benchmarks*
1/13-17	M. L. King, Jr.'s birthday	Transformational leaders	Write persuasive letter
1/20-24		Transformational leaders	Write compare/ contrast letter

The alternative form shows the four main subjects taught by elementary teachers in one column and the units indicated for each week. Though it lacks some of the details of the standard form, its chief advantage is that it shows how the several subjects relate to each other.

TABLE 12.2 Alternative Form, Elementary

Team: 5th grade   Date submitted: 9/23

Weeks/Subjects	*1/13-17*	*1/20-24*	*1/27-3*
Language arts	Opinion letter		
Social studies	Great leaders		
Science	Life in winter		
Math	Factoring		

2. *Provide the training.* One 2-hour training session for the entire faculty should be sufficient to introduce the form and review the skills needed. Follow-up sessions can be held at the team level. The next section of this chapter can provide the knowledge base for staff development.

3. *Establish deadlines for submission of plans.* Some principals with whom I have worked report that the following approach is highly effective: Recommend to teachers that, in the summer, they develop standard plans for the first four weeks of school. Use those four weeks to assess student

readiness, determine student needs, go over class routines, and introduce the subject. Then, with this knowledge of the students and the curriculum in mind, develop a sound plan for the rest of the year.

4. *Provide blocks of planning time for teams to collaborate on the planning.* With all these preparations made, one half-day work session should be sufficient to accomplish the planning process.

Developing Yearly Plans

There are several processes that teams can use in developing the yearly plan. Several teams have found the following one to be effective and efficient. (The process assumes that the team is using the form shown in Table 12.1 to plan one subject.)

1. *Complete the basic information.* The team should note the team's name, list the weeks of the school year, and note the important events.

2. *Identify the titles of the units to be taught.* The unit title should indicate the main focus of the unit. Four steps are involved here. First, the team should analyze the curriculum guide carefully, listing the mastery benchmarks in the order in which they are presented in the guide. The team should asterisk the objectives likely to be tested in state and district tests.

Next, the team should determine the organizing principle to be used in grouping the mastery benchmarks. The objectives have probably been listed in the guide according to some logical categorization of general goals. They may use this goal-based classification system or one of these alternatives: complex skills (Writing the Personal Narrative), time periods (The Industrial Age), themes (Families First), problems (Cleaning Up the Environment), major works of art (The Book of Job), or literary or artistic genres (The Nature of Tragedy).

The next step in identifying unit titles is to check the texts to be used. Teachers who have a somewhat shallow knowledge of the subject may find the textbook organization the simplest way to identify unit titles.

Finally, the team should make a tentative list of unit titles and then refine it through discussion and assessment. The titles should then be noted on the form.

3. *Determine the sequence of units.* Once the tentative list of titles has been developed, the team should next decide on the order of units. Several sequencing principles are available. Units can be organized according to

students' interests, beginning with a unit that has high interest and using seasonal progression to determine placement of other units. Second, they can be organized according to content difficulty, starting with units that are relatively simple and then moving to more challenging ones. Third, they can be ordered chronologically, as they often are in history courses or courses emphasizing British or American literature. They can also be organized in an "expanding horizons" approach, beginning with the individual, then the family, then the community, followed by the state and the nation. Finally, they can be organized in relation to the structure of that subject, as mathematics units usually are. Obviously, a team could also combine two or more of these principles.

4. *Allocate time to each unit.* The time can perhaps best be represented by the number of instructional periods to be devoted to the unit; an instructional period is defined as a clearly demarcated session lasting from 30 to 50 minutes. This is how the team should proceed:

- Calculate the total number of instructional periods available.
- Determine the relative importance of each unit, according to district and school priorities.
- Consider the attention span of the students.
- Assess the complexity of the unit, keeping in mind the importance of depth.
- Tentatively allocate periods to each unit.
- Translate the periods to lessons and to weeks.

5. *Record information on a yearly calendar.* All of the above information should be recorded on a yearly calendar.

6. *Relate curriculum guide mastery benchmarks to units.* Do one final check to be sure that all the mastery skills and knowledge have been included in the units. Perhaps the easiest way to do this is to note in the curriculum guide in which unit each mastery benchmark is emphasized.

Review the Plans

Once the grade-level or subject team has produced and evaluated their calendar, the principal should undertake his or her own review. The first step

TABLE 12.3 Criteria for Evaluating Yearly Calendars

Does the yearly planning calendar . . .
Reflect and correspond with the school calendar?
Note significant events likely to influence teaching and learning?
Organize the objectives into units, with titles clearly stated?
Sequence the units appropriately?
Allocate time appropriately?
Ensure that all mastery benchmarks are included?
Reflect the importance of depth of understanding?

---

is to review the calendars individually, using the criteria listed in Table 12.3.

Once all the individual calendars have been reviewed, the principal should examine all the calendars for a given grade level to see if there is appropriate correlation between related subjects such as science and mathematics and English language arts and social studies. Then the principal should examine all the calendars for a given subject to assess the grade-to-grade progression, ensuring that there is no undue repetition.

References

Clark, C. M., & Peterson, P. L. (1986). Teachers' thought processes. In M. C. Wittrock (Ed.), *Handbook of research on teaching* (3rd ed., pp. 255-296). New York: Macmillan.

Schmidt, W. H., Porter, A. C., Floden, R. E., Freeman, D. J., & Schwille, J. R. (1987). Four patterns of teacher content decision making. *Journal of Curriculum Studies, 19,* 439-455.

13

Developing Units of Study

With the yearly planning calendar developed, teachers are ready to move to the next level of planning—the unit. This chapter begins with a rationale for unit development, suggests a systematic way to organize teachers for unit development, and explains in detail a process for developing units based on constructivist principles.

A Rationale for Unit Development

Many teachers never move beyond short-term planning: They plan for one week or one day at a time. As a result, their teaching often seems fragmented and disjointed. Many principals reinforce this emphasis on short-term planning by checking daily lesson plans, ignoring the need to help teachers develop units.

Instead, principals should help teachers develop units, because unit planning has several advantages. First, unit planning stresses the holistic nature of learning: Students see the big picture rather than bits and pieces that do not seem to fit together. Second, the unit is the best level for integrating the curriculum. Whereas individual lessons can be integrated, the unit structure, in its emphasis on general concepts and themes, is a more effective vehicle for integration. Units also provide the best means for emphasizing skills across the curriculum—reading, writing, and studying. These skills—useful in most subjects—are easier to build into a unit structure rather than leave as stand-alone lessons. Also, the unit is the optimal level for enabling students to develop and apply problem-solving skills. Solving complex problems by drawing on a deep knowledge base takes time. Finally, the unit lends itself to the use of authentic assessment measures. Most units should culminate in the demonstration of learning.

Some teachers will resist an emphasis on unit planning. The reasons are understandable. Unit planning is more difficult than daily lesson planning, requiring skills that many teachers lack. Unit planning takes more time, a precious commodity for teachers. And in too many instances, unit planning seems to be a hit-or-miss process that teachers do in isolation, without help or encouragement. Principals need to take active leadership in helping teachers understand the importance of unit planning and in accomplishing the task in a more systematic manner.

Organizing for Unit Development

To avoid hit-or-miss planning, principals should develop the structures and plans needed for long-term systematic development. One suggested process is explained below.

Lay the Foundations

Begin by establishing a central planning group or assigning the central planning responsibilities to an existing committee or council. That group should complete the following steps:

1. *Identify the resources needed and develop a proposal to secure them.* Long-term unit planning will require resources—time, funds, materials, and expertise. Although funds are always limited, the planning group should work with the principal to develop a proposal for special funding from a variety of sources: the school board, federal and state programs, foundations, and parent organizations.

2. *Organize unit development teams.* At the outset at least, all teachers should be involved in a team approach to unit development. Later on, if teachers prefer to work independently, they may do so. In the initial stage, however, they will profit more from interaction and collaboration with col-

leagues. In elementary and middle schools, the teams will probably be organized by grade level; in high school, by subject.

3. *Decide how quality time can best be provided.* Teachers are not likely to produce quality units if they are required to do so after a long day of teaching. Instead, they need quality time. How this can be provided without unduly reducing instructional time is a complicated matter for the planners to consider, examining alternatives such as summer workshops, early dismissals, inservice days, and common planning periods.

4. *Provide the initial training needed to help teams get started.* Staff development to support unit planning should be an ongoing process rather than a one-shot intervention. The initial phase should concentrate on the skills teachers will need to begin their work effectively.

Make the Basic Decisions

The planning group should next make the basic decisions needed to get the project off the ground. They should secure teacher input in resolving the following issues:

- *What standard format should we use?* Although the specifics of format will vary from school to school, all units should include the following basic information: name and address of school district, name and address of school, title of unit, names of developers, date of publication, and grade level and subject.
- *What content criteria should we use?* One good way to promote quality is to establish and reinforce specific content criteria. Table 13.1 provides a suggested list.
- *Shall we begin with mastery or enrichment units?* The recommendation here is to begin with mastery, adding enrichment if there is sufficient time and interest.
- *Shall we begin with subject-focused or integrated units?* The answer will depend, of course, on the school's decision about integration, as explained in Chapter 9. In general, it is better to begin with subject-focused units because they are easier to develop.
- *What review process shall we employ?* All units should first be reviewed by the team of developers. They should then be submitted to the central planning group for further evaluation.
- *What storage-and-retrieval system shall we use?* If the school has the know-how and the software needed, store units in the computer. Otherwise, develop a central library accessible to teachers.

TABLE 13.1 Content Criteria

All units developed for Morris Middle School students will include the following:
A clear statement of the unit goal or the general outcome to be achieved
Time allocation for teaching the unit
Benchmarks and specific learning objectives derived from the goal
Learning activities that will enable students to achieve the objectives
Suggestions for remediating learning
Resources for the unit
Methods for assessing student learning

- *What schedule can be implemented for accomplishing the project?* A realistic schedule, showing for each grade or subject the units to be developed and the deadlines for developing them, will help keep the project moving.

Developing Units Based on Constructivist Principles

There are many models of unit development that teams can use in their planning. However, principals and teachers are strongly encouraged to use a constructivist model, as it is strongly supported by current research in cognitive psychology. *Constructivism* emphasizes the learner as an active maker or constructor of meaning and places contextualized problem solving at the center of all learning. The following discussion first reviews the basic principles of constructivism and then presents in greater detail a process for developing units based on a constructivist perspective.

The Basic Principles of Constructivism

Although each expert conceptualizes constructivism from a slightly different perspective, certain general principles can be synthesized from the literature. The discussion below draws from the following sources: Berryman (1991); Brooks and Brooks (1993); Collins, Brown, and Newman (1989); Marzano (1992); and Spielberger (1992).

The Nature of Learning

In considering the nature of learning, constructivism posits nine basic tenets:

1. Learning is not a passive receptive process but is instead an active meaning-making process. It is the ability to perform complex cognitive tasks that require the active use and application of knowledge in solving meaningful problems.

2. Thus, learning at its best involves conceptual change—modifying one's previous understanding of concepts so that they are more complex and more valid. Typically, the learner begins with a naive or inaccurate concept; the learning process enables the learner to develop a deeper or truer understanding of the concept.

3. In this sense, learning is always subjective and personal. The learner best learns when he or she can internalize what is being learned, representing it through learner-generated symbols, metaphors, images, graphics, and models.

4. Learning is also situated or contextualized. Students carry out tasks and solve problems that resemble the nature of those tasks in the real world. Rather than doing "exercises" out of context, the students learn to solve contextualized problems.

5. Learning is social. Learning at its best develops from interaction with others as perceptions are shared, information is exchanged, and problems are solved collaboratively.

6. Learning is affective. Cognition and affect are closely related. The extent and nature of learning are influenced by the following affective elements: self-awareness and beliefs about one's abilities, clarity and strength of learning goals, personal expectations, general states of mind, and motivation to learn.

7. The nature of the learning task is crucial. The best learning tasks are characterized by these features: optimal difficulty in relation to the learner's development, relevancy to the learner's needs, authenticity with respect to the real world, and challenge and novelty for the learner.

8. Learning is strongly influenced by the learner's development. Learners move through identifiable stages of physical, intellectual, emotional, and social growth that affect what can be learned and in what depth of understanding. Learners seem to do best when the learning is at their proximal stage of development, challenging enough to require them to stretch but attainable with effort.

9. Learning at its best involves metacognition, reflecting about one's learning throughout the entire learning process.

The Role of the Teacher

Constructivism also requires a change in the teacher's role. In the constructivist approach, the teacher carries out six essential functions, as Collins et al. (1989) note.

The first function is modeling: The teacher performs the task so that the students can observe and build a conceptual model of the processes. The second is coaching: The teacher observes the students as they carry out a task and offers hints, feedback, and modeling. The next teacher function is scaffolding and fading. *Scaffolding* is a metaphor for cognitive structure. At the initial stages of the learning process, the learner seems to function best with high structure, using teacher-provided cues, specific explanations, and organizing strategies to make sense of the problem and to engage in its solution. As the learner progresses, he or she needs less scaffolding; the goal is to *fade* gradually to turn over the entire process to the learner so that he or she becomes self-regulating.

The fourth teacher role is articulation: The teacher helps the students articulate their knowledge and their reasoning processes to make the cognitive processes visible. Reflection also is a key part of the teacher's role. The teacher helps the students reflect about their processes and compare them with those of an expert or another student. Finally, the teacher uses exploration, pushing students to do problem solving on their own, to frame questions, and to find answers.

The Importance and Nature of Problem Solving

The construction of knowledge best comes about when the learner is confronted with meaningful problems that must be solved. Rather than learning isolated so-called thinking skills, the learner more typically becomes engaged in solving meaningful problems that require him or her to use generative knowledge and to apply certain problem-solving strategies. This results in contextualized knowledge—knowledge that is understood in the context of meaningful tasks.

Problem solving as a general approach can be analyzed into several types. The following draws from and modifies the typology suggested by Marzano (1992):

- Decision making: Decision making answers the question, "What should we do?" or, "What should have been done?"
- Investigation: Investigation attempts to answer the general question, "What happened?" It can take several forms: How did this happen and why? What might have happened if . . . ? What will happen?
- Experimental inquiry: Experimental inquiry answers the question, "How can this phenomenon be explained?" It is the chief method of the empirical sciences.
- Problem solving: Problem solving as a specific type involves identifying how a remote goal can be achieved by overcoming obstacles, such as "How can we reduce the consumption of fossil fuels?"
- Invention: Invention is the generation of something that fills an unmet need. It is the use of creativity in fashioning a new product or a new approach.

As the learner is solving problems, he or she is experiencing a "cognitive apprenticeship"; by observing and imitating the teacher or more sophisticated peers, the learner is expanding his or her repertoire of problem-solving skills, testing knowledge claims, and developing greater understanding.

Developing Units From
a Constructivist Perspective

This issue of unit development is so critical that it requires closer examination. As noted above, there are many models of unit development. The following discussion explicates one process that embodies constructivist principles; the model has worked well in curriculum workshops presented for classroom teachers. (For purposes of greater clarity and directness, the second person *you* is used in this section to represent the unit planning team.) Though the steps below are listed in linear fashion, they should be seen as flexible and recursive. Developers can start at any point in the process and move back and forth recursively.

To guide the process of unit development, you should keep in mind the criteria shown in Table 13.2 and use them to guide your work and evaluate the products. The criteria have been derived from the literature on unit development, modified to accommodate the special nature of constructivism. (The following sources provide useful guidance for the unit development process: Bethke, 1985; Ellis, Mackey, & Glenn, 1988; Glatthorn, 1987; Perkins & Blythe, 1994.)

Block in the Unit. The first step is to *block in the unit.* The blocking process establishes the general parameters within which the unit will be developed. You make several decisions—or confirm some decisions previously made.

- *The title of the unit.* The title should make clear the general emphasis of the unit. The unit being used as an example here will be called *Our Changing Language.*
- *The length of the unit.* If you have not previously decided about the length of the unit, you should do so at this stage, keeping in mind the importance of curriculum depth. Obviously you will also consider the students' development stage and attention span. A general rule of thumb is this: The older the student, the longer the unit. In the example chosen, you might tentatively allocate two weeks to this language unit.
- *The unit goal or outcomes.* Each unit should have one to four clearly stated major goals or outcomes. A shorter unit will probably have one goal; longer units may have as many as four. The unit goal is a general statement of what you want the students to learn by studying the unit. Unlike the benchmarks and the more specific lesson objectives, the unit goal will often be stated somewhat generally. To ensure a problem-solving orientation, you might consider using language that clearly implies a critical thinking or problem-solving orientation. Here are some examples: Think critically about television, solve a problem relating to language change, use concepts of semiotics to interpret the culture critically, understand the ecology of the tundra, understand climate change and predict changes, understand how families are changing and predict further changes.

Identify the Problem to Be Solved. In this approach to unit development, you or the students identify a problem or a set of problems to be solved in the unit. It should be noted that some curriculum experts with a constructivist orientation take a different direction here: For example,

TABLE 13.2 Special Criteria for Constructivist Units

The unit is outcomes focused: The unit goal or key outcome is clearly stated; the benchmarks and the lesson objectives are directly related to the unit goal or standard.

The unit makes appropriate integration of content from that subject (or from two or more subjects) and makes use of writing and reading as ways of learning.

The unit emphasizes depth, not superficiality, with sufficient time provided to achieve depth of understanding.

The unit focuses on problem solving, conceptual change, and critical thinking, in the context of real situations.

The unit has appropriate sequence and coherence so that lessons build on and relate to each other.

The unit fosters a constructivist approach to learning, one that sees the learner as an active maker of meaning and a cognitive apprentice, using generative knowledge to solve meaningful problems.

The unit emphasizes a social context for learning, with effective use of cooperative learning and student interaction.

The learning activities recommended are directly related to the outcomes, are likely to achieve the outcomes, and are developmentally appropriate.

The unit makes appropriate provisions for individual differences and is especially sensitive to the needs and strengths of students from minority ethnic groups.

The unit provides for authentic assessment of learning.

Perkins and Blythe (1994) recommend that at this stage you should identify a "generative topic"—a topic that is central to the discipline, accessible to the students, and connectable to diverse topics within and outside the discipline. That generative topic is then used to derive the goals of the unit. The problem focus seems to provide a more direct route to the goal of problem solving.

There are several ways that problems can be identified. First, problems can often be derived from the unit goals, benchmarks, or more specific grade-level objectives in the curriculum guide. As you review them, you will begin to see interesting problems emerge. You can also think of questions that can lead to problems. Here the heuristics shown in Table 13.3

TABLE 13.3 Heuristics for Identifying Problems

What is its nature?
   1. What is it?
   2. What does it mean?
   3. What is its structure? How can we make a model of it? What are its parts?
   4. How would you classify it?
   5. What different perspectives do people have about it?
   6. How does it operate?
   7. What patterns can be seen in its various manifestations?
   8. What is wrong with it, and how would you fix it?
What are its relationships?
   9. What are its similarities and differences with others in its class?
  10. What is its quality in comparison with others?
  11. What inferences and generalizations can be drawn from it?
  12. What are its causes and its effects?
  13. How and why is it changing?
  14. What were its past forms, what are its present forms, and what will be its future forms?
What are the options with respect to it?
  15. What are your values with respect to it?
  16. How can it be improved?
  17. What are your choices with respect to it?
  18. What new forms or uses of it can we create?

---

may help you. You can apply those heuristics in two ways. You can apply them to a set of themes or concepts, such as the following: family, friends, culture, conflict, regions and places, ethnic groups and genders, eras and ages, environments, and careers. Thus, using Heuristic 5 (What different perspectives do people have about it?) in connection with the theme *careers,* you could identify this problem:

> How do the following people view the role of the principal? The principal? The teachers? The students? The parents? The superintendent? The school board?

You can use those same heuristics in examining the several components of the subject or subjects you are focusing on. For example, you can apply Heuristic 13 to the study of communication to identify this problem:

How are electronic media (such as the computer) affecting the way we communicate?

You can also focus on the students by having them generate questions that they would like to answer. In facilitating this process, you may wish to teach them a simplified version of those same heuristics. After students list several specific questions they would like to answer, you can assist them in grouping the individual questions into problem statements.

Another way to identify a problem is to begin with the materials available. Problem-solving units work best when students can gain access to and use a body of knowledge. If you have a good collection of materials on a topic such as advertising, you can review it to see what problems it suggests.

After tentatively identifying the problem to be solved, reflect about the unit goal previously identified. Now consider several factors: the time available, the students' knowledge and interests, and the materials available. This reflection process may suggest the need to reframe the unit goal—to modify its general thrust or to make the outcome more sharply focused. In the example analyzed here, the problem of language change seems too broad and demanding for eighth-grade students, particularly considering that only two weeks have been allocated to the unit.

The unit outcome might be reframed in this manner:

Explain how and why the vocabulary of the language changes.

Draft the Unit Scenario. The next step is one not ordinarily found in curriculum texts, but it has been found to be especially effective in working with classroom teachers. The *unit scenario* is a script for the unit. It explains in general form how the unit begins, how it moves through the stages of learning, and how it ends. It includes some reference to the major ways the students will learn, emphasizing how they will solve the central problem. In brief, before you get into the details of the lesson objectives and activities, you delineate the big picture.

Develop the scenario by first reflecting, imagining, and brainstorming in a somewhat freewheeling manner. As ideas crystallize, jot them down, continuing in this manner until you have a very clear mental picture of the major components and flow of the unit. The final step is to write a clear draft that can guide you and your colleagues. Here is the first draft of the unit scenario for the unit on vocabulary change:

Activate students' prior knowledge by asking them how they think new words come into the language. Then have students interview grandparents on words used today that were not used when they were in high school, such as *laser*. Have them use the results to make some preliminary generalizations. Maybe then set up expert groups, each one studying in depth one way that words come into the language. After studying how, move into why—technology, societal changes, immigration patterns. Then have them predict some new words for the year 2010. Close by having expert groups present a report and students do a role play of teenagers talking in the year 2010.

When you have finished the first draft of the scenario, you should check it against the criteria for unit excellence. This is only a preliminary check to ensure that you are moving in the right direction.

Developing the unit scenario is a very useful mental process to assist in planning. In many ways, the mental processes are more important than the writing. And the unit scenario helps you do the mental planning. However, the scenario need not be included in the unit itself.

Determine Knowledge Needed and Means of Access. With the scenario in mind, think about the knowledge needed and how students will gain access to that knowledge. Students can best solve problems when they have in-depth knowledge relative to the problem. In this sense, this unit model synthesizes content and process rather than seeing them as separate entities. Students acquire knowledge—and then make that knowledge generative in solving the problem. To identify the knowledge needed, reflect on the scenario and then focus on the problem, asking this question: "If I were solving the problem, what knowledge would I need?" Then adapt your knowledge needs to the students' developmental level.

To solve the problem of vocabulary change, students would probably need to have access to two bodies of knowledge: the types of vocabulary change and the factors that affect vocabulary change.

Also, think about the most efficient and effective means for the students to get access to that knowledge. In making this decision, consider the age of the students, the nature of the knowledge, and the materials readily available—or those that you are able to produce. Here are several ways that students can access knowledge: Listen to the teacher present information; learn through guided discovery and discussion; interview experts, parents, and other sources; learn from peers; read texts and other print materials; use computer software; view television; and use other media.

These resources for knowledge acquisition provide the raw materials for problem solving; they embody the generative knowledge that students will need to solve the problem. All problem-solving units will require the students to gain access to and use such knowledge resources. Some teachers have found it useful to identify resources early in the unit planning process, because knowledge resources play such a critical role.

In the unit planned here, the following resources might prove useful: collections of new words that have recently come into the language, short stories from several periods of our history illustrating vocabulary change, articles bewailing and welcoming vocabulary change, teacher-written materials on vocabulary change.

Consider How Students Will Solve the Problem. Students should be taught the problem-solving process they will need to solve the problem and then have an opportunity to apply it, both individually and in groups. In the example here, students would need to be taught the principles of inductive reasoning and the skills of predicting.

Determine Which Learning Strategies They Will Need to Learn. Learning strategies are the mental operations that help in the problem-solving process. Some are generic, such as using Web diagrams to suggest connections; some are subject specific, such as listing all the known elements in solving mathematical problems. Such strategies are better taught in context, not in isolation.

Determine How Students Will Demonstrate Learning. An important piece of the planning process is to decide how students will demonstrate their learning. In fact, experts have pointed out that planning can often begin by deciding how learning can be authentically assessed—and then proceed by "teaching to the test." The demonstration may take many forms: publications, dramatizations, visual displays, reports, and essays. The essential issue is to ensure that the demonstration of learning is closely related to the goals of the unit.

As noted in the scenario, the demonstration in the unit used as an example would take two forms: Groups would report on how words come into the language, and students would role-play, using new words they predict would enter the language.

Sketch in the Lesson Plans. With the unit-level planning completed, you now move to the lesson level. But you don't develop lessons *de novo.* You develop them from all the work you have done thus far at the unit planning level. Thus, a lesson is derived from the unit; a unit is not a random collection of lessons. As you develop lessons, keep the focus on problem solving and conceptual change, using generative knowledge.

Prepare the Unit for Review and Dissemination. The final step is to prepare the unit for peer review and dissemination. Systematize all the previous decisions, add the necessary details, and prepare a review draft for

Table 13.4 Form for Unit Planning and Dissemination

TITLE OF UNIT _____ GRADE LEVEL _____
DEVELOPERS _____
UNIT GOAL _____
STANDARD _____
BENCHMARKS _____
PROBLEM _____

UNIT COMPONENT	LESSON 1	LESSON 2	LESSON 3	LESSON 4
LESSON OBJECTIVES				
KNOWLEDGE SOURCE				
PROBLEM SOLVING				
LEARNING STRATEGY				
ASSESSMENT				

colleagues to evaluate the unit. Teachers have found the form shown in Table 13.4 useful in systematizing these decisions. The form lists down the left the major components of the unit; across the top, it lists the daily lessons. Thus, a three-week unit would list 15 daily lessons. (Only a portion of the unit is shown.) The use of the form has several advantages: It reminds developers and users of the major components of the unit. Viewed from left to right, it shows how a given component develops across the unit. Viewed from top to bottom, it shows the main elements of the daily lesson plan.

A Concluding Note

Constructivism seems to be more than another fad; it represents a significant break from behaviorist models of teaching and learning, a relatively new approach that will probably grow in influence. However, to be effective it will require curriculum workers to rethink the nature of curriculum units and the processes used to develop units based on a constructivist perspective.

References

Berryman, S. E. (1991). *Cognitive science: Challenging schools to design effective learning environments.* New York: Institute on Education and the Economy, Columbia University.

Bethke, E. (1985). *A guide to curriculum planning: Purposes and procedures.* Madison: Wisconsin Department of Public Instruction.

Brooks, J. G., & Brooks, M. G. (1993). *The case for constructivist classrooms.* Alexandria, VA: Association for Supervision and Curriculum Development.

Collins, A., Brown, J. S., & Newman, S. (1989). Cognitive apprenticeships: Teaching the craft of reading, writing, and mathematics. In L. B. Resnick (Ed.), *Knowing, learning, and instruction: Essays in honor of Robert Glaser.* Hillsdale, NJ: Lawrence Erlbaum.

Ellis, A. K., Mackey, J. A., & Glenn, A. D. (1988). *The school curriculum.* Needham Heights, MA: Allyn & Bacon.

Glatthorn, A. A. (1987). *Curriculum leadership.* New York: HarperCollins.

Marzano, R. J. (1992). *A different kind of classroom: Teaching with dimensions of learning.* Alexandria, VA: Association for Supervision and Curriculum Development.

Perkins, D., & Blythe, T. (1994). Putting understanding up front. *Educational Leadership, 51*(5), 4-7.

Spielberger, C. D. (1992). Learner-centered psychological principles: Guidelines for school redesign and reform. *Psychology Teacher Network, 2*(2), 5-12.

14

Enriching the Curriculum and Remediating Learning

As district leaders develop the curriculum and as teachers make yearly planning calendars, they should both be aware of the need for the enrichment and remediation that occur at the classroom level. The principal can play a key role in helping teachers develop quality enrichment materials and remediate learning effectively.

Helping Teachers Enrich the Curriculum

Enrichment is defined here as learning that goes beyond and extends the mastery curriculum. The mastery curriculum is the core curriculum that meets these criteria: It is essential for all students, it is best learned with a great deal of structure, and it is the curriculum likely to be tested. It is the curriculum that the district controls. The mastery curriculum should be designed by the district so that it does not require more than 80% of the time available. The remaining time can then be used by teachers for enrichment and remediation. In this way, all students experience an enriched curriculum, rather than it being offered only to the gifted (who need it least of all).

The Nature of the Enrichment Curriculum

The enrichment curriculum lacks the essentiality and importance of the mastery curriculum, but it needs careful planning, primarily to avoid excessive repetition from grade to grade. The enrichment curriculum should be seen as the leaven of the curriculum, providing lightness and excitement and restoring some fun to the curriculum.

Content for the enrichment curriculum can be derived from several sources, as follows:

- Special student interests
- Special teacher knowledge and interests
- Aspects of that discipline not typically studied in school
- New developments in the subject
- Special knowledge of parents and other community members
- Local aspects of a topic that is drawn from the mastery curriculum
- Topics in the mastery curriculum studied in greater depth

Because it is less important, the development of the enrichment curriculum should take a lower priority than the development of mastery units.

General Planning for the Enrichment Curriculum

The first step is to develop school-based policies and general procedures for the enrichment component. Here are the issues to be considered:

1. Will the enrichment content be delivered as part of regular courses, or will it be organized as an elective course? If elective courses are used as the means of delivery, how will credits be assigned at the secondary level?

2. How much time should be allocated to enrichment? Will enrichment be offered during the regular class period, before school, after school, during a special class period, or in special "enrichment weeks" carved out of the school calendar?

3. Who, besides certified teachers, can teach enrichment content: school administrators, district supervisors, aides, parents, other community volunteers, students, university faculty? What policies will govern the use of noncertified personnel?

4. What resources will be provided to support enrichment learning?

The next step is to organize multigrade teams for every subject that will use enrichment units. At the higher grade levels, students can provide useful input for such teams. The task of these teams is to develop for that subject a master chart similar to the one shown in Table 14.1. Even in elementary schools using a grade-level organization, the multigrade, single-subject perspective is needed at the outset of the project.

A central committee composed of teachers, school administrators, and parents should then review these proposals, checking for the following:

- Do the proposed units enrich the curriculum?
- Are the proposed units developmentally appropriate?
- Do the proposed units avoid repetition?
- Are the proposed units likely to be approved by parents?
- Do the proposed units respond to the special needs of our students?
- Do the proposed units sufficiently provide for integration?

At this juncture, teachers will probably need one session devoted to the development of the enrichment curriculum. Although they can use the unit planning skills they have acquired, they should be encouraged to see the enrichment curriculum as a special opportunity to be creative. Unlike the mastery curriculum, it need not be objectives driven, tightly structured, and carefully assessed. The enrichment curriculum is a time for them to try new approaches, test new materials, and bring to bear their special knowledge and interests.

To provide a climate that will stimulate teacher creativity, teachers should be assured that they will not be evaluated while presenting the enrichment curriculum. One simple way of preventing inappropriate evaluation is for the teacher to post a simple "Enrichment" sign when an enrichment lesson is being presented.

Evaluating the Enrichment Curriculum

Though teachers should not be evaluated while presenting the enrichment curriculum, the principal should work with them in assessing the impact of the enrichment curriculum. The assessment should include three major components.

First, a committee should review all proposals and all enrichment units to ensure the necessary quality. Second, peers should give each other nonevaluative feedback as they observe each other teach enrichment units. Finally, students should be surveyed from time to time to assess student perceptions of quality.

TABLE 14.1 Enrichment Planning for Social Studies

GRADES: 6-8
PLANNERS: Harley, Washington, Garcia
OVERALL DESIGN:

In social studies, the enrichment units will be organized as mini-courses requiring six periods of instruction. Students will select one course from the three listed; parent approval will be necessary.

PROPOSED UNITS:
Grade 6
Shopping can be dangerous to your health (integrated unit combining economics and health education)
Watching town council in action (civics and political science)
Centreville in the Civil War (local history)
Grade 7
Eating across the world (introduction to anthropology)
Understanding groups in action (elementary sociology)
Ordinary heroes (multicultural education and history)
Grade 8
Watching the stock market (economics)
The economics of clean air (integrated unit combining science and economics)
You, the beach, and the sea (geography)

Helping Teachers Remediate Learning

In implementing the curriculum, teachers should work for mastery by all students. To accomplish this goal, they will need to develop their expertise with two kinds of remediation: on-the-spot remediation and systematic remediation.

On-the-Spot Remediation

On-the-spot remediation is the response the teacher makes in every lesson when he or she is aware that students are not mastering the content. The principal should ensure that teachers understand this simple process.

Frequently Monitor Student Learning

In every class, teachers should monitor learning on an ongoing basis. The monitoring can take many forms: observing students at work, evaluating student products, asking questions, interpreting nonverbal signals of confusion, encouraging student questions, having students write brief statements of what they are learning, and giving brief written quizzes.

Adjust Instruction as Needed

When the monitoring suggests that several students are not mastering the content, the teacher should make the necessary adjustments. These can take many forms, including the following:

- Using a simpler vocabulary to explain key concepts
- Giving more examples of concepts
- Using visual representations of the concept
- Taking additional time to explain
- Providing students with concrete experiences with the concept
- Using students who have mastered the concept to explain it in their words

In observing instruction, principals should assess the teacher's skill in on-the-spot remediation and provide whatever help is needed.

Systematic Remediation

Systematic remediation is a structured program designed to increase the performance of low-achieving students who need more help than that provided by on-the-spot remediation. By reviewing grades, test scores, and other indices of learning, the principal should work with the teachers in identifying students who need systematic remediation.

Rather than adopting some quick-fix program, the principal should work with teachers in a problem-solving mode. Here they can use those factors identified from the research and shown in Table 14.2. Brief explanations of the factors follow.

Three of the factors involve out-of-school elements. The first is the extent of parental involvement and support. When parents provide a supportive learning environment at home and become actively involved with the school, student achievement is improved. The second is how students spend out-of-school time. If they spend too many hours watching television and working for pay and too little time doing homework, achievement will suffer. The final out-of-school factor is peer pressure. Especially among minority youth, school achievement is perceived as selling out to the majority culture. Peers will often ridicule students who work hard to achieve.

TABLE 14.2 Factors Accounting for Student Learning

Student factors
  1. Student age
  2. Student ability
  3. Student motivation
School factors
  4. Curriculum
  5. Instruction
  6. Use of in-school time
  7. School and classroom climate
Out-of-school factors
  8. Parent involvement
  9. Peer pressure
 10. Use of out-of-school time

SOURCE: Adapted from Fraser, Walberg, Welch, and Hattie (1987).

Seven factors involve the school. Three of these relate to the student as a learner. The student's age and developmental maturity influence learning; to a great extent, this is outside the school's control. The student's ability in a subject and prior achievement in that subject also influence learning. The final factor is the student's motivation to learn that subject. Low motivation means less learning.

Two are climate factors. The overall school climate influences learning: Students need an environment that is safe, orderly, and learning focused. The classroom climate, in general, should emphasize a task orientation, high expectations for all students, and sufficient warmth to make students feel known and valued.

The three remaining factors are under the direct control of the school. The first is the amount of time that students are actively engaged in learning. The second is the effectiveness of the teaching methods used: Too much teacher talk results in less attention and less learning. The final element is the quality of the curriculum and its potential for engaging students in learning.

The principal and teachers can use the results of this problem analysis to design a systematic enrichment program. A typical program that addresses several of these factors would include the following strategies:

  1. Providing additional time after school
  2. Using volunteers as afterschool tutors

3. Using materials that provide an alternative route to learning
4. Working with parents to develop a supportive home environment
5. Providing staff development for all teachers on making the curriculum more meaningful and using more effective teaching strategies

A Concluding Note

Teachers should understand that simply implementing the standard curriculum is not enough. They need to enrich the curriculum for all students and provide enrichment as needed.

Reference

Fraser, B. J., Walberg, H. J., Welch, W. W., & Hattie, J. A. (1987). Syntheses of educational productivity research. *International Journal of Education, 11,* 145-252.

15

Evaluating the Curriculum

The curriculum should be evaluated at every step of its development. In determining a schedule for development, the task force should conduct a needs assessment. When the scope and sequence chart is in draft form, they should evaluate it rigorously for consistency, focus, and coordination. As the new guide is developed in draft form, they should evaluate it. The most important evaluation, however, will occur at the school and classroom levels as the principal and teachers cooperate in a rigorous evaluation of curriculum quality. If the evaluation is to be useful, however, it should employ a comprehensive framework that includes all the teacher-relevant curricula explained in Chapter 10: the assessed or tested curriculum, the supported curriculum, the written curriculum, the taught curriculum, and the learned curriculum.

Evaluating the Assessed or Tested Curriculum

The assessed or tested curriculum usually includes four kinds of tests or assessments of student learning: standardized tests, state tests, district tests, and classroom tests. In evaluating the first three types, the teachers should find that the alignment process explained in Chapter 10 is sufficient evaluation. The single issue here is the extent of congruence between the test and the written curriculum. If the alignment process indicates a major lack of congruence between these tests and the written curriculum, the district has a clear choice: Change the test or change the curriculum.

Helping Teachers Develop and Evaluate Classroom Tests

Teachers will need the assistance of the principal in developing and evaluating classroom tests. If the principal can help teachers develop more valid classroom tests, both can rely on test results with greater confidence. Developing valid and reliable classroom tests is an important and complex skill. Its complexity is exemplified in a 17-step flowchart developed by Nitko (1983) that shows all the steps that should be taken by test makers in developing a valid achievement test.

Though the process he describes is useful in developing major departmental examinations that have major impact on the student's educational future, it is perhaps too complex and time-consuming for making classroom unit tests. What follows, then, is a simplified process that will result in better tests.

The first step is to assess the constraints and resources. This first step examines some practical considerations—what constraints will place limits on the nature of the test? and What resources are available to help the teacher develop the test?

The second step is to analyze what was taught. There are two useful ways of analyzing what was taught. Berliner (1987) recommends that the teacher develop a two-dimensional matrix for this analysis. Down the left-hand side the teacher lists the content areas. For example, the content areas for a unit on the Civil War might include these: causes of the war, alignment of states in the war, significant battles in the war, people who played key roles in the war, and results of the war. Across the top, the matrix classifies the desired behaviors of students. Berliner uses three classifications: knowledge/comprehension, application, and analysis/synthesis/application. The teacher then uses the matrix to identify foci for test items. Thus, the intersection of the content area of *people who played key roles* with the desired behavior of *analysis/synthesis/evaluation* would yield this focus for a test item: *Evaluate Lee and Grant in relation to their effectiveness as generals.*

An alternative method that I have used with teachers is illustrated in Table 15.1. This method uses categories of objectives that seem more in keeping with the way teachers conceptualize units: terms, facts and infor-

TABLE 15.1   Unit Analysis Form

List the terms taught.

Natural resource, renewable resource, pollution, environment, conservation, water treatment plant, sewage treatment plant, phosphate, algae, solar energy

List the facts and information taught.

The Environmental Protection Agency is a government agency that monitors compliance with laws.

Taking a shower uses 95 liters of water; taking a bath uses 133 liters.

The manufacture of plastics requires the use of strong chemicals and high temperatures.

Between 1980 and 1985, the world population increased by about 550 million people.

List the big ideas taught.

The water cycle

Acid rain

List the skills and processes taught.

Interpret a table of data.

Identify common causes of air pollution.

List the learning strategies and problem-solving skills taught.

Analyze the trade-off involved in requiring factories to reduce pollution—cleaner air results in higher prices for the consumer.

Explain how one person can make a difference in conservation.

---

mation, big ideas, skills and processes, critical thinking, and problem solving. It serves the same purpose as the content/behavior matrix; it simply uses different categories.

The unit analysis form can be distributed to students to help them prepare for the test; it can also be used by the teacher as a means of guiding the review work.

Next, determine which objectives will be tested. Most teachers do not want to take the classroom time needed to test everything that appears in the analysis of what was taught. They should select from the complete list those items that they believe should be tested, considering elements such as the importance of that item for future work, the amount of time that was devoted to teaching it, the resources available, and the time required for testing it.

The fourth step is to determine relative weights for all objectives to be tested. The weights serve three purposes: They help the teacher prepare the test; they help the student allocate time during the test; and they aid the teacher in scoring the test. The easiest way to indicate relative weights is with a percentage figure.

Next, write the test items. The information collected thus far is now used to write test items. The teacher first determines the type of questions to be used for each objective, weighing both issues of validity (which type will most validly assess learning?) and utility (which type will be easiest to score?).

Here there are several choices: essay question, fill-in-the-blank, or supply-the-answer; true-false; matching; multiple choice; performance or demonstration. Each of these has its own advantages and limitations. Essay questions best tap the ability to reason but are difficult to score. Fill-in-the-blank and supply-the-answer are best for sampling knowledge but are a bit more time-consuming than other short-answer types, for both the student and the teacher.

True-false are easy to score, but they permit guessing and also do not validly assess many objectives that cannot be so dichotomized. Matching and multiple choice are useful short-answer types but again involve a guessing factor. As explained more fully below, performance tests probably yield more valid information about learning but are difficult to construct and score.

The next step is to assemble the test and write the directions. In assembling the test, the teacher has several choices about how questions should be ordered and grouped. The teacher can group by content; for example, all the questions dealing with the battles of the Civil War could be grouped together. The teacher could group by behavior desired, gathering all the knowledge-comprehension items together. Bloom, Hastings, and Madaus (1971) recommend that when the items are relatively homogeneous with respect to content and behavior, it might be desirable to group by difficulty, beginning with the easier questions. They also note that when different kinds of items are used (such as true-false, multiple choice), it is probably wise to group by type. Doing so makes it easier for the teacher to give directions and the student to follow them.

The final step is to write clear directions. Test developers should use simple language that the students can read and understand. They should write full directions, not relying on the explanations given orally when administering the test. They should also indicate the point value. Here are examples of unclear and clear directions:

Unclear: Match the names of the generals with the battles they led.

Clear: Below are listed five generals. Each has a blank space next to his name. Find in the list below the battle that he led. In the blank space, write the letter that is next to the battle he led.

Example:

Jones: d   (10 points)

Now the teachers are ready to review and revise the test. They should give the test to a colleague and ask him or her to identify any potential problems. They should also review the test to be sure that the directions are clear. As a final check, they should take the test themselves to determine the time required and the clarity of directions.

To emphasize the importance of quality classroom tests, the principal should schedule a conference with each teacher and use that conference to examine collaboratively a test that the teacher has given and graded and one that the teacher plans to give. The criteria shown in Table 15.2 can be used by the teacher in developing classroom tests and by the principal in assessing their quality.

Helping Teachers Evaluate
by Assessing Performance

Because of growing dissatisfaction with paper-and-pencil tests, educators are increasingly exploring the use of performance, exhibition, or demonstration assessment, in which the student is asked to perform or demonstrate competence. Such performance or demonstration measures are typically recommended for evaluation at several levels: at the end of the unit, at the end of the term or year, and at the end of some level of schooling, such as middle or high school.

Sizer (1984) believes that a high school diploma should be awarded on the basis of what he terms an "exhibition of mastery," which requires the student to demonstrate real intellectual accomplishments. Such exhibitions, as he describes them, would be public performances at which the student would prove that he or she had mastered certain broad skills and knowledge bases.

Here, for example, is a performance test that could be used in grades K through 4 in mathematics. Students are given a large box of raisins and are asked to estimate the number of raisins in it. To accomplish the task, they are provided with a balance, containers of different sizes, and a calculator. They must use a second method to check their first estimate and record the results. (This test was cited by Mitchell, 1992, as based on the standards of the National Council of Teachers of Mathematics.)

Wiggins (1989) identifies eight intellectual design features of such demonstrations: essential (not just for a grade), enabling (point the learner toward more complex use of skills), contextualized and complex (not discrete skills taken out of context), involving student research, assessing habits and repertoires (not recall or "plug-in" skills), representative (emphasizing depth, not breadth), engaging and educational, and involving ambiguous tasks.

Though the art of developing demonstrations or performance measures is relatively recent, some preliminary writings in the field suggest that a process like the following would be used (for a fuller discussion of the process, see Archibald & Newmann, 1988; Stiggins, 1987; Wiggins, 1998).

The initial step is for developers to identify a major educational goal they want the student to achieve at the end of a certain level of schooling. The goal should be a general one that encompasses several component skills and knowledge bases; it should also have educational significance. Suppose, for example, that they wanted all eighth graders to have achieved this goal: become a more discriminating and critical user of television.

Next, they should analyze that goal into its constituent behaviors—the more specific behaviors that constitute the general goal. This second step will assist in developing the demonstration measures. As they complete this second step, they should keep in mind both the developmental level of the learners and the limits of what is attainable in schooling.

Here, for example, are the constituent behaviors that might be identified for the general goal given earlier:

- Limit television viewing to no more than 12 hours a week.
- Use selection tools (such as critics' columns and newspaper schedules) to identify important shows to watch.
- Demonstrate an awareness of how commercials attempt to shape behavior by appealing to basic human drives and needs.
- Evaluate television news shows for objectivity and fairness.

Now the developers should identify the demonstrations or performances required for the student to exhibit mastery. Wiggins (1989) suggests seven structural features here: involve a public; do not rely on arbitrary time constraints; offer known tasks; provide cumulative evidence, such as a portfolio; require collaboration; encourage practicing; make feedback central.

Here are the demonstrations or performances that the teachers might require for the critical viewing goal identified earlier:

1. You are to present to the class two logs of television viewing: one showing your viewing schedule at the beginning of the school year; the second, at the end of the school year. You will explain to the class the major differences between the two logs.

TABLE 15.2 Criteria for Evaluating Classroom Tests

Format, Style, Directions
  Does the test have a professional appearance and use a clear format?
  Is the test written clearly and correctly, free of spelling, punctuation, and
    gramatical errors?
  Are the directions clear?
  Are point values clearly stated?
Content
  Is the test comprehensive, sampling all areas covered in the unit?
  Do test items include all levels of complexity, from comprehension to
    synthesis?
  Does the weighting of test items reflect the importance of the content?
  Do the form and wording of items minimize opportunities for guessing?

---

2. You and four of your classmates will be given a copy of the entertainment section of the Sunday newspaper and a copy of *Newsweek* magazine for the same week. You will be expected to identify five shows that you consider important to watch and explain why you have chosen them.

3. You will be shown videotapes of three commercials for a popular brand of athletic shoes. You will explain in a well-written essay how those commercials are attempting to influence your buying behavior.

The final step is to devise the rubrics. The rubrics are an evaluation guide that lists the levels of performance and the features desired at each level. Then the developers can write a scoring plan to be used in evaluating the performance, including the score recording method to be used. Stiggins (1987) identifies these score recording methods as possibilities: checklist, rating scale, anecdotal record, portfolio, audio- or videotape.

Though some have questioned the practicality of such complex performance measures, they do seem to be a very promising alternative to paper-and-pencil objective tests.

Evaluating the Supported Curriculum

The supported curriculum includes all the learning materials used to support the written curriculum, including texts and software. Here again, the alignment process can be useful in determining the congruence between the supported and the written. If major gaps are found to exist, three options are available: purchase other materials, change the curriculum, or develop supplementary materials to fill the gap.

If the principal and the teachers have an opportunity to participate in the selection process, they can use the criteria shown in Table 15.3 to make a more systematic assessment of quality.

Evaluating the Written Curriculum

The written curriculum includes the scope and sequence chart and the district curriculum guide. When the district developers have produced the first draft of the scope and sequence chart for a given subject, principals and teachers should evaluate it critically, as it provides a foundation for the more detailed curriculum guide. They should use the criteria shown in Table 15.4 as a basis for their assessment.

The curriculum guide itself can be evaluated by using the criteria shown in Table 5.1 in Chapter 5.

Evaluating the Taught Curriculum

The taught curriculum is the curriculum that the teacher actually delivers. An evaluation of the taught curriculum should use three approaches. First, as explained in Chapter 12, the principal should cooperate with the teacher in assessing the yearly plan, using the criteria shown in Table 12.3. Second, the principal should collaborate with the teacher in reviewing the units developed, using the criteria shown in Table 13.2 in Chapter 13.

Finally, periodic observations should be made to determine the extent to which the teacher presents lessons that are derived from these yearly and unit plans and to assess the effectiveness of the delivery. These observations will be of three types. First, as explained in Chapter 11, informal observations should be made periodically as a means of monitoring the curriculum. Second, any formal evaluation of teaching by the principal should include one item that refers to implementation of the curriculum; observations for evaluation purposes should include an assessment of this component. Here is the way such a criterion might be stated: *Implements the district curriculum with fidelity and effectiveness.*

All these observations should be limited to an assessment of the mastery curriculum. As noted in Chapter 14, the teacher's delivery of the enrichment curriculum should not be evaluated.

TABLE 15.3 Criteria for Evaluating the Supported Curriculum

Format, Appearance, Durability
   Are the materials of high quality in their physical make-up: clear in format, attractive to the eye, made of durable materials?
Style
   Are the materials readable by intended users but not oversimplified?
   Are the materials free of bias based on gender, ethnicity, and age?
Content
   Does the content suitably reflect the nation's cultural diversity?
   Does the copyright date indicate that the content is current?
   Is the content congruent with the curriculum?
   Does the content provide sufficient depth for the topics treated?
Authorship
   Does the authorship include both scholars in the field and experienced classroom teachers?
Evaluation
   Have the materials been rigorously field tested?

Finally, peers can observe each other and then give objective, nonevaluative feedback focusing on delivery of the curriculum. Such peer observations can be a regular part of a more comprehensive peer coaching program that enables the teacher to be observed to determine what the observation will include (see Glatthorn, 1990, for fuller details here). Or they can be specifically organized for the purpose of evaluating the curriculum as one phase of a comprehensive curriculum evaluation.

The peer observations for curriculum implementation should give the teacher feedback about this issue alone, addressing three specific issues:

- Was the lesson part of a unit that was based on the district curriculum?
- Did the teacher make clear how the lesson related to the overall unit, providing appropriate reviews, linking the present lesson with lessons previously taught, and showing the connections with what is to come?
- Did the teacher help the students connect with the content, showing the relevance of the content to their own lives?

TABLE 15.4 Criteria for Evaluating Scope and Sequence Chart

Does the chart suitably reflect the recommendations of experts and professional groups?

Does the chart correspond with state standards and state tests, where applicable?

Is the chart easy to read and interpret, without excessive detail?

Does the chart focus on mastery outcomes?

Is the grade placement developmentally appropriate?

Do the entries reflect systematic development, without excessive repetition?

Do the entries indicate effective coordination from grade to grade and level to level?

Evaluating the Learned Curriculum

The most important evaluation question to ask examines the learned curriculum: Have students achieved the learning goals of the curriculum? Two types of evaluation are useful here.

Assessing Student Learning in Every Class

Principals should help teachers assess student learning as a part of every class session. One of the most important uses of evaluation is to guide the instructional process. In this sense, evaluation is not perceived as something separate from instruction; instead, it is conceptualized as an integral part of teaching. In almost every lesson, the effective teacher uses an interactive and recursive process: assess-plan-teach-assess-modify plans-teach. The research on effective monitoring of student learning suggests that the following practices can be used in almost every lesson. (The discussion that follows draws primarily from Berliner, 1987; Bloom, Hastings, & Madaus, 1971; Good & Brophy, 1987; Guskey, 1985; Jacobs, 1995. To facilitate its use, it is written as a handout that might be given to teachers.)

First, begin the instructional session with a brief oral or written quiz that checks students' knowledge of skills and knowledge taught in prior lessons. If you use a written quiz, have students check their own work or each other's, emphasizing that the quiz has only an instructional purpose for you and them. If you use oral quizzing, keep your questions and responses brief.

Second, as you explain a concept or skill, monitor attentiveness by observing student behavior, remembering that such monitoring does not always yield reliable results. Do not be misled by students who have mastered the art of concealing inattentiveness by giving signals of being on task.

Next, after you have explained a concept or demonstrated a skill, check for students' understanding. The easiest way is to ask a few specific questions, being sure not to call on only those who volunteer. You can ask younger students to use certain previously established signals, such as "thumbs up/thumbs down" or " hold up one finger if the first answer is correct, two if the second." Or with reluctant or less able students, you can ask for a group response.

If you assign seatwork or have students work in groups, monitor their work closely as they learn and, as noted above, hold them accountable for the productive use of time.

Also, from time to time, evaluate their learning by asking them to write a brief response to a question or to explain their understanding of a concept. Such written responses help students clarify their own understandings and give you useful feedback.

Finally, close class with a brief evaluation of what has been learned. You can use several methods for this end-of-class evaluation—conducting a brief oral quiz, using a written quiz, or requiring all students to write a summary of the lesson's highlights.

In addition to using these guidelines for each class, keep in mind some general practices. First, remember that the primary purpose of such evaluation is to improve learning. Use errors as opportunities for learning. Second, follow up the instructional evaluation with appropriate feedback to the students and additional help when that is indicated. Third, use the evaluation to modify your own instructional approaches. You should remediate if students have not learned. If it is obvious that most of the students have not understood a concept you just explained, you should reteach, modifying the learning processes. Finally, build in as often as you can opportunities for student self-evaluation. You can give self-scoring quizzes. You can use special student response sheets that reveal the correct answer when the appropriate spot is rubbed. And the computer is ideal as an evaluation tool; it provides instant feedback and effective follow-up.

Evaluating Unit Achievement

The other approach to evaluating the learned curriculum is to analyze the results of end-of-unit tests. If the test has been developed by following the procedures explained previously, it should provide a valid measure of student learning. However, teachers will need help in analyzing and using test results as they typically do not take the time for such an approach. Because the analysis of unit test results can be a time-consuming process, principals may want to provide special staff development time for teachers to learn and practice the skill, using a unit test they have administered. The following process should work for most teachers.

1. Prepare a large chart. Across the top, list the major areas covered by the test. Here, for example, is how one teacher analyzed the coverage of a test on the Civil War:

- Causes of the war
- Alignment of the states
- Major battles and their outcomes
- People who played important roles in the war
- Results and effects of the war

Down the left-hand side of the chart, list the names of all the students in that class.

2. Record on the chart how each student performed on each section of the chart, using one of these symbols:

E: excellent performance
S: satisfactory performance
U: unsatisfactory performance

3. Analyze the results, examining both dimensions—which students, which areas.

4. On the basis of the analysis of results, use one of the following options:

- Provide for individual remediation if only a few students did not achieve mastery. Proceed with the next unit for the entire class.
- Provide for group remediation if several students did not achieve mastery. Delay introducing the new unit; let achievers work on enrichment content.
- Reteach the whole class as needed if most of the students did not achieve mastery. Let achievers serve as peer tutors.

A Concluding Note

The curriculum evaluation process explained here is comprehensive but time-consuming. Principals should use it flexibly on the basis of their assessment of need and the immediate value of the results obtained.

References

Archibald, D., & Newmann, F. (1988). *Beyond standardized testing: Authentic academic achievement in the secondary school.* Reston, VA: National Association of Secondary School Principals.

Berliner, D. C. (1987). But do they understand? In V. Richardson-Koehler (Ed.), *Educators' handbook: A research perspective* (pp. 259-294). New York: Longman.

Bloom, B. S., Hastings, J. T., & Madaus, G. F. (1971). *Handbook on formative and summative evaluation of student learning.* New York: McGraw-Hill.

Glatthorn, A. A. (1990). *Supervisory leadership.* New York: HarperCollins.

Good, T. L., & Brophy, J. E. (1987). *Looking in classrooms* (4th ed.). New York: Harper & Row.

Guskey, T. R. (1985). *Implementing mastery learning.* Belmont, CA: Wadsworth.

Jacobs, H. H. (1995). *Mapping the big picture.* Alexandria, VA: Association for Supervision and Curriculum Development.

Mitchell, R. (1992). *Testing for learning.* New York: Free Press.

Nitko, A. (1983). *Educational tests and measurements: An introduction.* Orlando, FL: Harcourt Brace Jovanovich.

Sizer, T. (1984). *Horace's compromise: The dilemma of the American high school.* Boston: Houghton Mifflin.

Stiggins, R. J. (1987). *Design and development of performance assessments.* Washington, DC: National Council on Measurement in Education.

Wiggins, G. (1989). Teaching to the (authentic) test. *Educational Leadership, 46* (7), 41-47.

Wiggins, G. (1998). *Educative assessment.* Alexandria, VA: Association for Supervision and Curriculum Development.

PART

Looking Ahead

16

Curriculum Leadership: Putting It All Together

The preceding chapters have taken an analytical approach to curriculum leadership, examining the separate functions that should be accomplished. This chapter summarizes by suggesting how the principal can fit all these separate activities into an integrated process.

Work Closely With District Leadership

Though this work has been centrally concerned with curriculum work at the school level, it has also emphasized the critical role of the state and the district. It is especially important for the principal to work closely and collaboratively with district leadership in the ways indicated rather than acting independently. That close cooperation can perhaps best take place within a formal school-based management program. Though the research indicates that school-based management is not associated with student achievement, it seems to result in a higher level of innovation and has a positive effect on teacher morale, at least in the initial years (see Glatthorn, 1996).

Set Up the
Organizational Structures

With a cooperative relationship established with district leadership, the first step is to organize for curriculum improvement. Each school will have its own committee structure, but the one illustrated in Figure 16.1 has worked for many schools. A School Leadership Council serves as the central group, the basic decision-making body in a school-based management approach. It develops an overall school improvement plan that is revised each year. To carry out the curriculum-related tasks, a Curriculum Task Force is appointed. It works collaboratively with the Instructional Teams, which are organized by grade level in the elementary and middle schools and by department in the high school.

Use Team Leadership

Though this work has emphasized the importance of the principal's role, several reasons suggest the need for the team approach described in Chapter 3. First, a team approach makes the principal's job more manageable by spreading the tasks to others. Second, a team approach is an effective means of harnessing the talents of others rather than relying solely on the abilities of administrators. Finally, the team approach is more likely to build support among teachers by involving them in the decision making.

Make Curriculum Improvement
Part of an Overall Plan

Curriculum improvement will have its greatest impact if it is an integral part of an overall school improvement plan. Schools are complex interacting systems: Changing one aspect has a ripple effect on the remaining parts of the organization. An example is the current interest in the 90-minute block schedule. In one high school I audited, the school implemented a new block schedule without changing the curriculum or providing staff development to help teachers change the way they taught. The result was unfortunate: The teachers used the first 45 minutes to present the standard curriculum and then used the second block of time for student seatwork.

Use an Incremental Process
in Effecting Curricular Change

Though there are strong pressures for radical school improvement, the research indicates that incremental change is the most effective. Experts in

Figure 16.1. Organizational Structures

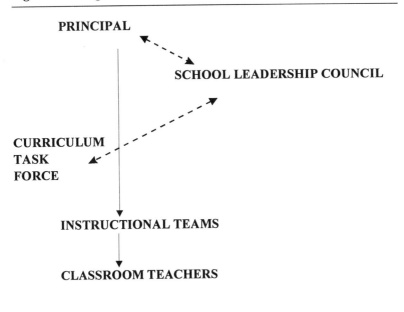

the change process who have reviewed the research conclude that the most effective change occurs when leaders hold big dreams and take small steps to accomplish them. After reviewing the history of high schools that had accomplished significant change, Louis and Miles (1990) concluded that it is best to start small, experiment, and expand the successful while contracting the less successful. The advice seems especially sound in considering curriculum change. Developing and implementing a new curriculum will take 2 to 3 years if high quality and effective implementation are to be achieved. The process cannot be hurried.

Prioritize Curriculum Tasks

The order in which curriculum tasks will be carried out will be determined by several factors: (a) the requirements of the school improvement plan, (b) the internal relationships of the functions, and (c) the school's special needs, among others. If the importance of the change is the sole criterion, the following priorities would be assigned:

High Priority

1. Develop the school's program of studies.
2. Develop a learning-centered schedule.

3. Monitor and assist in the implementation of curriculum.

Middle Priority

4. Align the curriculum.
5. Help teachers develop a yearly planning calendar.
6. Help teachers develop units of study.

Lower Priority

7. Develop the school's vision and goals.
8. Determine the nature and extent of curriculum integration.
9. Help teachers enrich the curriculum and remediate learning.
10. Help teachers evaluate the curriculum.

Use Routine Activities to Support Quality Curricula

The evidence indicates that effective principals carry out the same tasks as less effective principals (Lee, 1987). The difference is that effective principals use these routine activities as a means of fostering school improvement; less effective principals carry out those same activities in a mindless manner. Here are some examples of the ways that principals could use routine activities to support the curriculum:

- While monitoring the student cafeteria, ask students about their perceptions of what they are studying.
- In making informal observations, focus on curriculum implementation.
- Organize informal lunch seminars with teachers to discuss current curricular issues.
- When report cards have been issued, talk informally with teachers about the impact of curriculum on student achievement.
- In evaluating teacher performance, include an analysis of the teacher's implementation of the curriculum.
- Use a part of each faculty meeting as an opportunity to support the new curriculum.

Develop Specific Plans and Manage Time

Effective principals do their best to plan systematically and manage their time to accomplish their goals. They control their time, setting priorities and blocking the time needed to accomplish their goals. Less effective principals move from crisis to crisis, without clear goals, letting others determine their schedules. They sit in the office, waiting for the next conference or crisis, as a steady stream of parents, teachers, and students consumes the time available. Though the unpredictability of school life makes it impossible to develop rigid plans and control all the hours of the principal's day, it is possible—and necessary—to set clear goals and build a flexible schedule that provides quality time for curriculum leadership.

To illustrate a process that can be used, assume that the School Leadership Council has assigned to the Curriculum Task Force the responsibility of planning and directing a project to renew the school's program of studies (see Chapter 7 for the details). Principal Marcia Howard works with the council in developing an action plan similar to the one shown in Table 16.1.

TABLE 16.1 Action Plan: Renewing Program of Studies

General Goal: **To fine-tune the present program of studies so that it leads to a better educated student body.**

Actions	*Responsible*	*Start*	*Finish*
Secure initial approval of superintendent	Howard	8/1	9/1
Develop the knowledge base	Henrico	9/1	12/1
Disseminate, discuss knowledge base with faculty	Howard	1/5	1/12
Identify constraints, resources	Smiley	10/1	11/15
Design comprehensive evaluation	Howard	1/15	2/1
Carry out evaluation	Haskins	2/15	5/15
Review evaluation results and report to faculty	Henrico	6/1	6/15
Plan special workshop to develop proposed changes	Howard	6/30	7/1
Hold special workshop	Howard	8/15	
Prepare report for parent, superintendent, board review	Howard	10/1	10/30

Howard then reviews the plan and lists the tasks for which she is chiefly responsible:

- Secure initial approval of superintendent.
- Disseminate, discuss knowledge base with faculty.
- Design comprehensive evaluation.
- Plan special workshop to develop proposed changes.
- Hold special workshop.
- Prepare report for parent, superintendent, board review.

She notes the starting and finishing date for each responsibility. She then takes each major responsibility and analyzes it further into its component steps. Thus, for the first step, she makes this mental list of what has to be done, knowing the superintendent's decision-making style:

1. Write memo to superintendent requesting conference and summarizing tentative plans.
2. Schedule conference with superintendent.
3. Hold conference.
4. Write follow-up memo.

For each of those specific steps, she assigns a target date and enters that in her planner.

The planning styles of individual principals will vary, of course. The important concerns are to set specific goals, analyze them into actions to be taken, and build a schedule that will accomplish them.

A Personal and Concluding Note

I view this book chiefly as a practical handbook for principals and assistant principals that spells out the leadership skills needed to establish a quality school-based curriculum. Yet the book should not be concluded without emphasizing the leadership dispositions and attitudes needed to inspire and cooperate with classroom teachers—the prime deliverer of the curriculum. Those attitudes discussed below may be much more important than any set of skills.

A Determination to Act Ethically. At the time of writing this revised edition, several articles appeared in the national press reporting massive cheating by principals who fraudulently changed and falsely reported test results. Predictably, excuses were offered by the principals and their supporters: too much emphasis on test scores, fear that their schools would look bad, concern for disadvantaged minority students. However, there is no excuse for unethical behavior. In all things, act ethically.

A Focus on Results. All that really matters is the learned curriculum. Even the taught curriculum should be seen as a facilitating element, not as the primary goal. However, from my perspective, legitimate results go beyond test scores. These student outcomes, among others, also matter: increased motivation to learn; a positive attitude toward the school, the teachers, and other students; the ability to resolve conflicts productively; a disposition to act ethically.

A Belief in Teachers. Although there are too many teachers with low motivation and an excess of self-concern, my 54 years of teaching have persuaded me that an overwhelming majority of teachers are conscientious professionals who want the best for the children and youth they teach. Curriculum development should be based on a foundation of trust: Teachers want to conform with state and district regulations; teachers want to be successful; teachers want to help all students achieve success; teachers want to produce quality curricula.

A Concern for Accountability. All those involved with the schools should be held accountable for their actions: the community, in providing support; the parents, in being productively involved; the school board, in developing learning-centered policies; district leaders, in fostering school-based decision making, developing and implementing a learning-centered budget, and training school administrators; school administrators, in providing learning-centered leadership; the teachers, in improving the quality of the curriculum and instruction; and the students, in making the best use of quality teaching. To limit accountability to principals and teachers is manifestly unfair and unwise. Principals and teachers should be held accountable for those elements they can control. But one of the elements that has the greatest impact on student achievement is educational financing, a factor over which principals and teachers have very little influence.

High Expectations for All. Leadership, curricula, instruction, and assessment should all be based on realistically high expectations for students—a sincere belief that all students want to learn and can learn. Those high expectations also apply for self, for teachers, and for parents. These are trying times for educators, when "teacher bashing" seems to be a popular indoor sport. Despite these antagonistic forces, all of us need to be realistic optimists who hope for the best and learn from the worst.

References

Glatthorn, A. A. (1996). *School based management: A policy analysis.* Greenville, NC: School of Education, East Carolina University.

Lee, G. V. (1987). Instructional leadership in a junior high school: Managing realities and creating opportunities. In W. Greenfield (Ed.), *Instructional leadership: Concepts, issues, and controversies* (pp. 77-99). Newton, MA: Allyn & Bacon.

Louis, K., & Miles, M. B. (1990). *Improving the urban high school: What works and why.* New York: Teachers College Press.

Index

CORWIN